THE CUTE BOOK OF
KAWAII
DRAWING

How to Draw 365 Cute Things, Step by Step

Woo! Jr. Kids Activities Founder: Wendy Piersall

Book Layout by: Lilia Garvin
Cover Illustration: Michael Koch
Interior Illustration: Avinash Saini

Published by DragonFruit, an imprint of Mango Publishing, a division of Mango Publishing Group, Inc.

For permission requests, please contact the publisher at:

Mango Publishing Group
2850 Douglas Road, 2nd Floor
Coral Gables, FL 33134 USA
info@mango.bz

For special orders, quantity sales, course adoptions and corporate sales, please email the publisher at sales@mango.bz. For trade and wholesale sales, please contact Ingram Publisher Services at customer.service@ingramcontent.com or +1.800.509.4887.

The Cute Book of Kawaii Drawing: How to Draw 365 Cute Things, Step by Step

ISBN: (p) 978-1-64250-701-0

HOW TO USE THIS BOOK

All you need is a pencil, an eraser, and a piece of paper!

Follow each drawing diagram step by step:

TIPS & TRICKS

Draw lightly at first, because you might need to erase some lines as you work.

Add details according to the diagrams, but don't worry about being perfect! Artists frequently make mistakes—they just find ways to make their mistakes look interesting. You can erase mistakes, or use them as a new decoration.

Don't worry if your drawings don't turn out quite the way you want them to. Just keep practicing! Sometimes drawing the same thing just a few times will help.

You can draw a new animal or object every day, or several each day. For an extra challenge, use your creativity to combine multiple drawings into an entire scene, like below, where a bunch of yummy foods decorate bakery shelves.

KAWAii BAKERY SCENE

CHOCOLATE CHIP COOKIE

SPRINKLE DONUTS

SLICE OF CAKE

MUFFIN

CITRUS CUPCAKE

ADDING COLOR!

Another way to decorate your drawings and scenes is to add color.
Did you know that there are different colors known as primary colors,
secondary colors, and tertiary colors? Let's check them out!

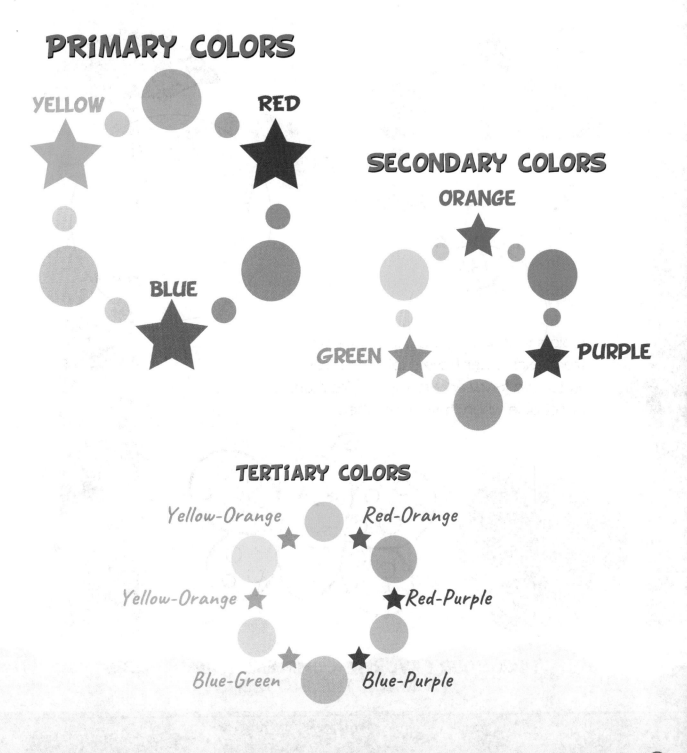

PRIMARY COLORS

YELLOW

RED

BLUE

SECONDARY COLORS

ORANGE

GREEN

PURPLE

TERTIARY COLORS

Yellow-Orange

Red-Orange

Yellow-Orange

Red-Purple

Blue-Green

Blue-Purple

COMPLEMENTARY COLORS

One simple way to find colors that look very good together is to draw
a line straight across the color wheel. Let's take a look!

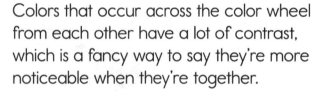

Colors that occur across the color wheel
from each other have a lot of contrast,
which is a fancy way to say they're more
noticeable when they're together.

Orange...
& Blue

Green...
& Red

Purple...
& Yellow

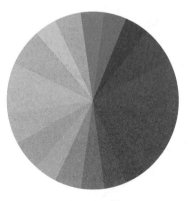 

PICK YOUR FAVORITE COMPLEMENTARY COLORS
& COLOR THE BUTTERFLY!

LET'S PRACTICE BLENDING!

Analagous colors are special colors that appear next to each other. For example, one group of adjacent analagous colors is orange, orange-red, and red. Another is green, light-green, and yellow.

To explore analagous colors, let's try blending from one color to another! First we'll go from orange to red, then purple to blue, and finally yellow to green.

Orange... ▶▶▶ ...Red

NOW, YOUR TURN!

Purple... ▶▶▶ ...Blue

Yellow... ▶▶▶ ...Green

DRAWING NEW FACES

Congratulations! You're a kawaii artist now.

Every artist gets to make decisions about the cute things they draw. We're going to practice personalizing drawings.

Check out these cute bees!

Notice how changing their expression gives them each a different personality.

Every drawing you make can be changed to be unique!

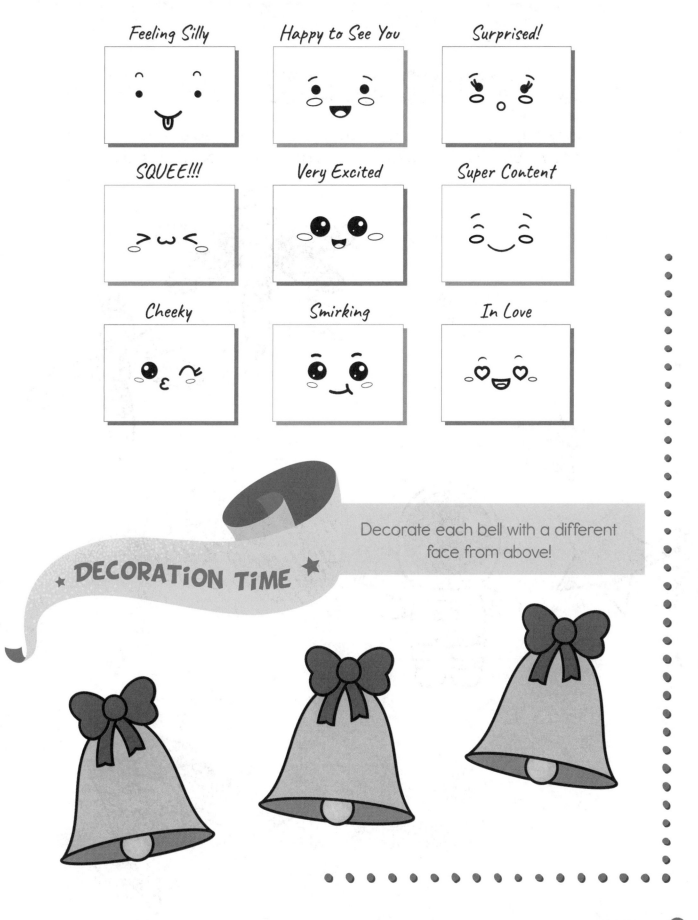

Feeling Silly

Happy to See You

Surprised!

SQUEE!!!

Very Excited

Super Content

Cheeky

Smirking

In Love

★ DECORATION TIME ★

Decorate each bell with a different face from above!

MAKE YOUR DRAWINGS POP!

Creativity is the special spark that makes your drawings so unique! Here are a few suggestions on details you can add to any doodle or scene.

Give your kawaii drawings a friend!

Add some stars!

Add a splash of color behind your drawing, and decorate with hearts!

Add clouds and a sun for an outdoor scene!

Give your fun fuzzy friends little wiggle lines!

Add water bubbles to cute underwater critters!

YOU'RE READY TO DRAW!

♥ Remember to have fun! ♥♥

IN THE YARD

Watering Can — — — — — — — — — — — — — —

Grass — — — — — — — — — — — — — —

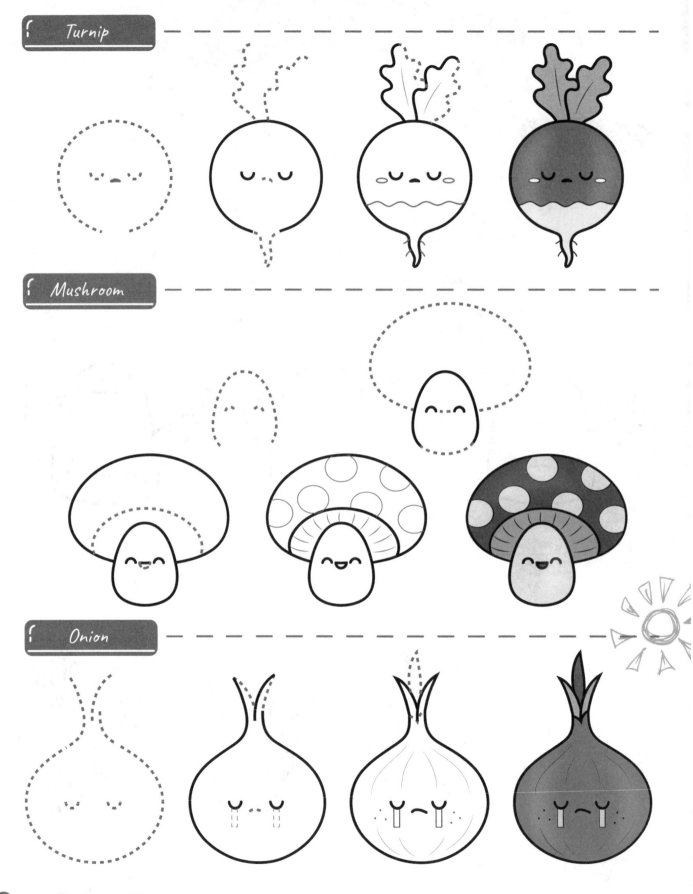

Turnip

Mushroom

Onion

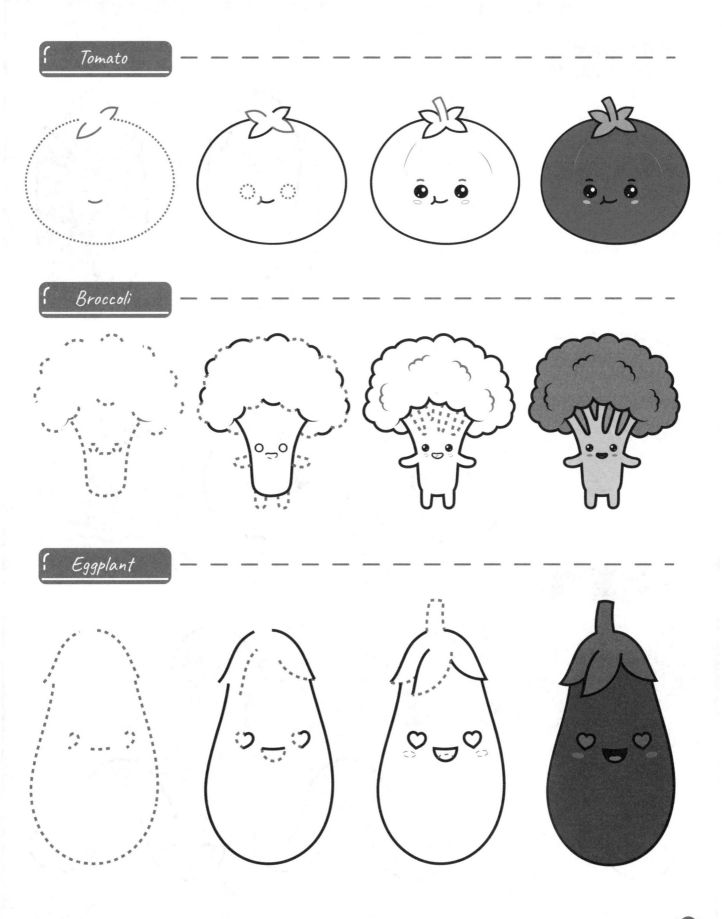

Tomato

Broccoli

Eggplant

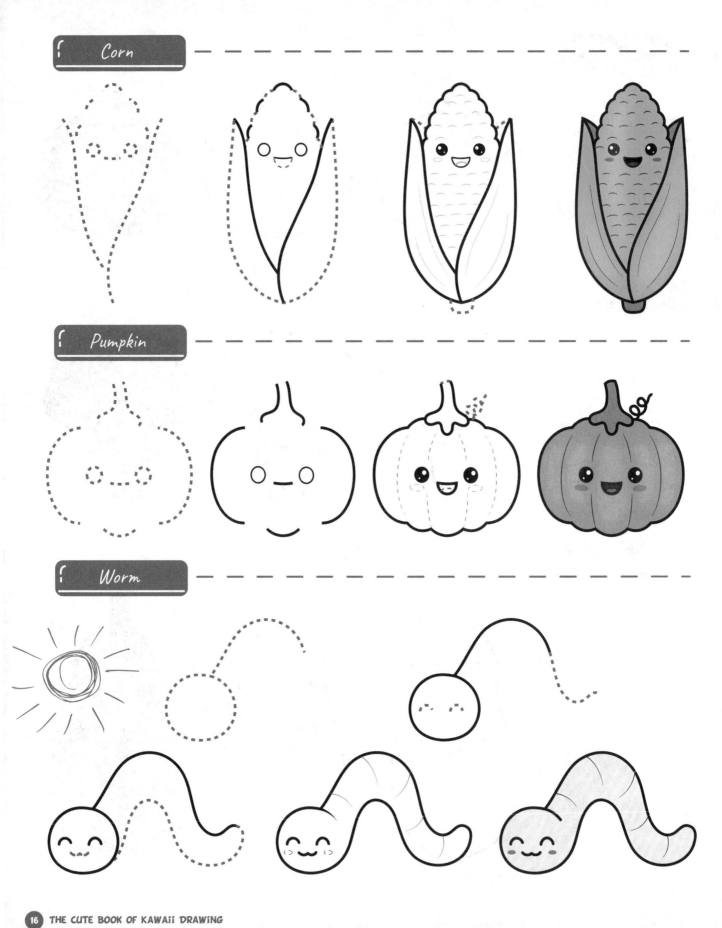

Corn

Pumpkin

Worm

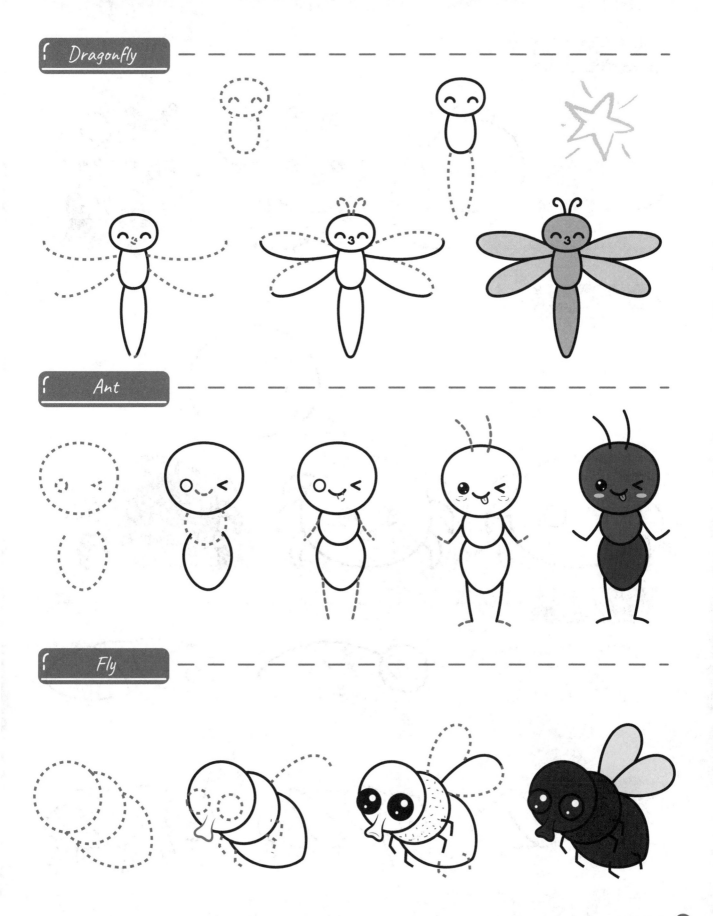

Dragonfly

Ant

Fly

Bumblebee

Fuzzy Spider

Cricket

Butterfly

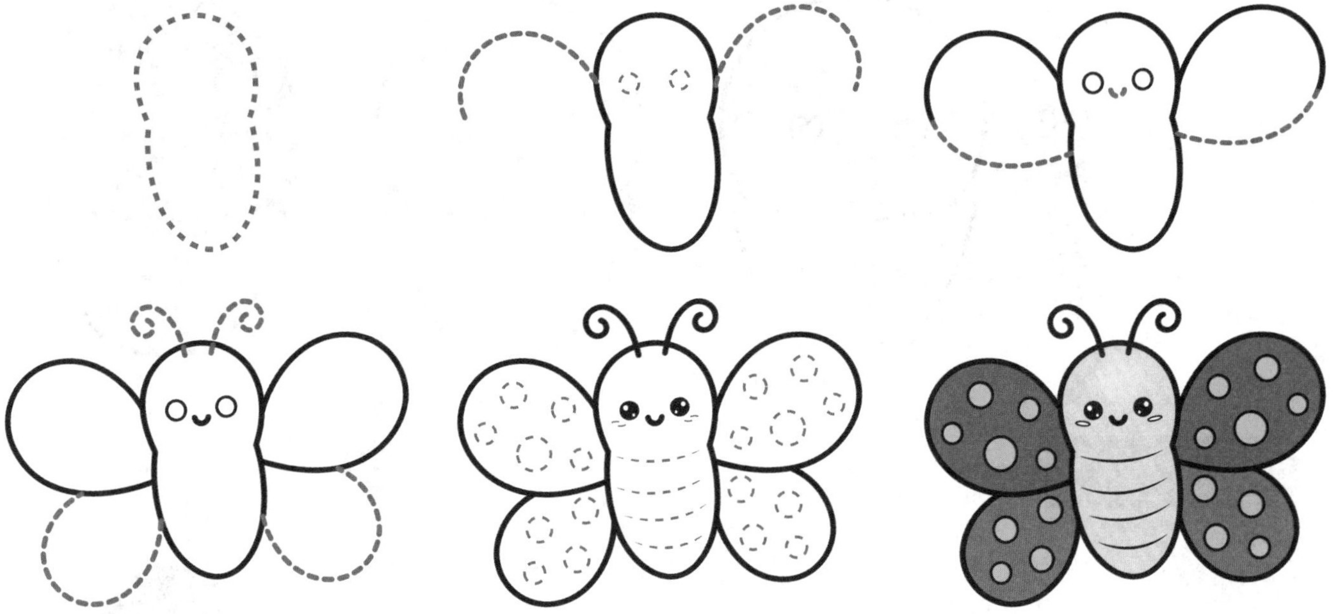

Ladybug

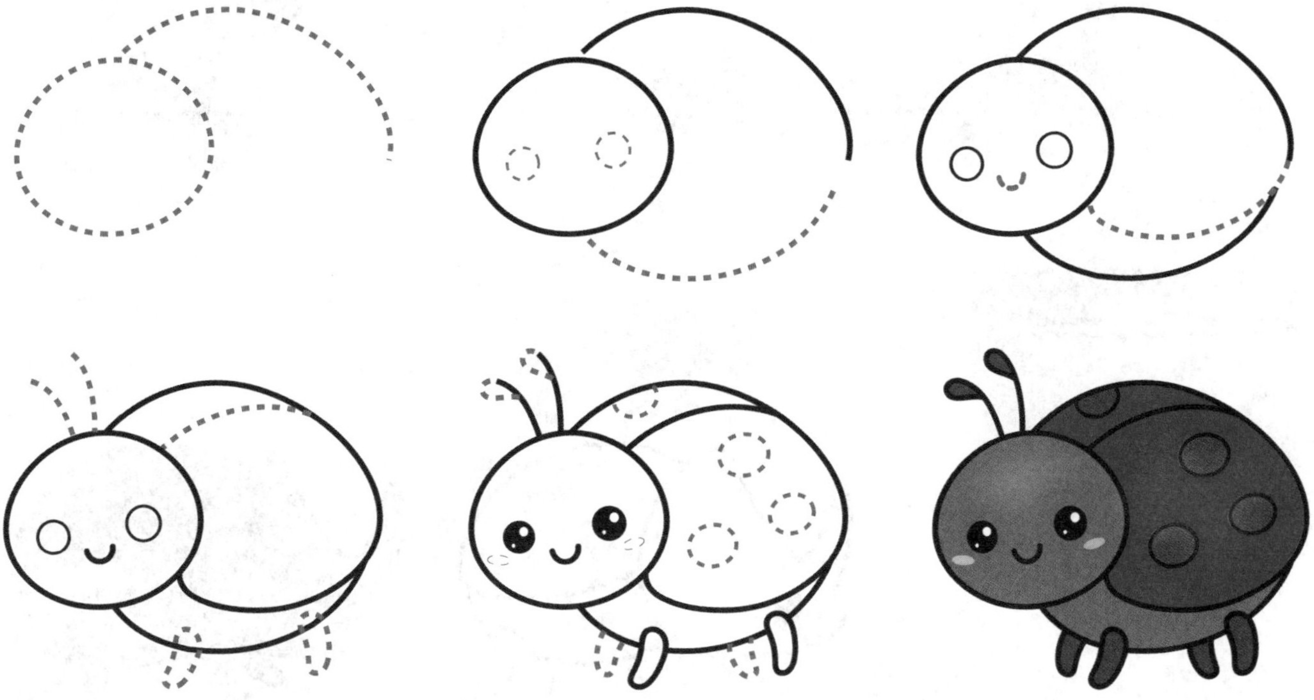

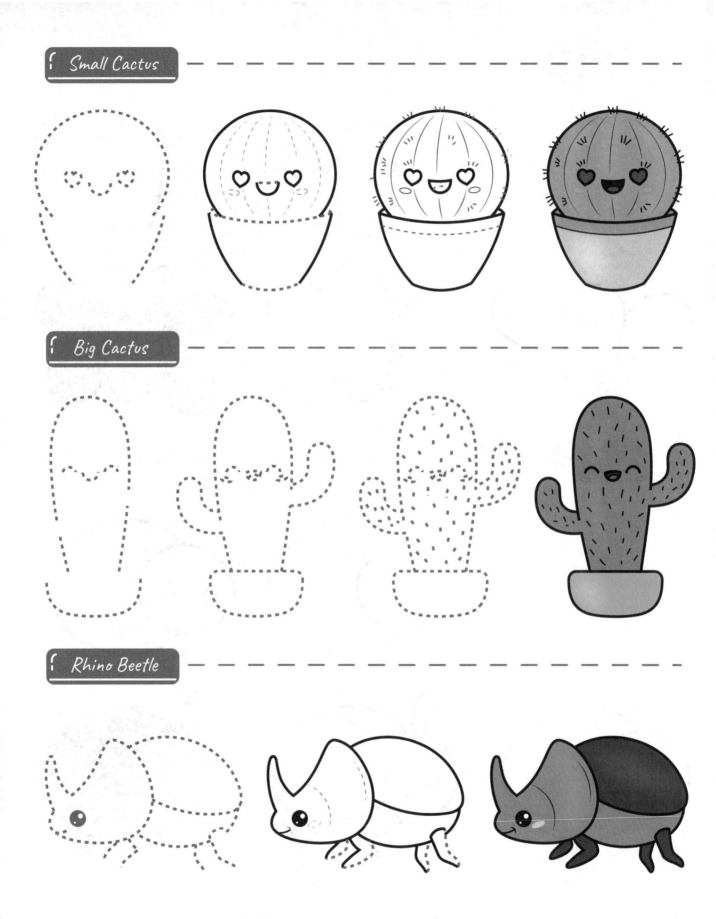

Small Cactus

Big Cactus

Rhino Beetle

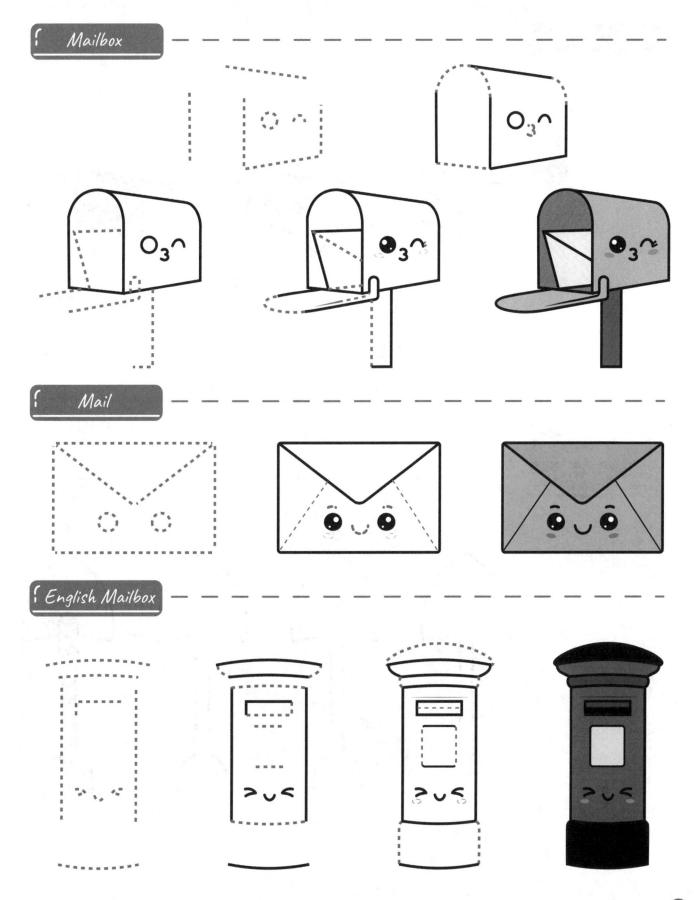

Mailbox

Mail

English Mailbox

Handaxe

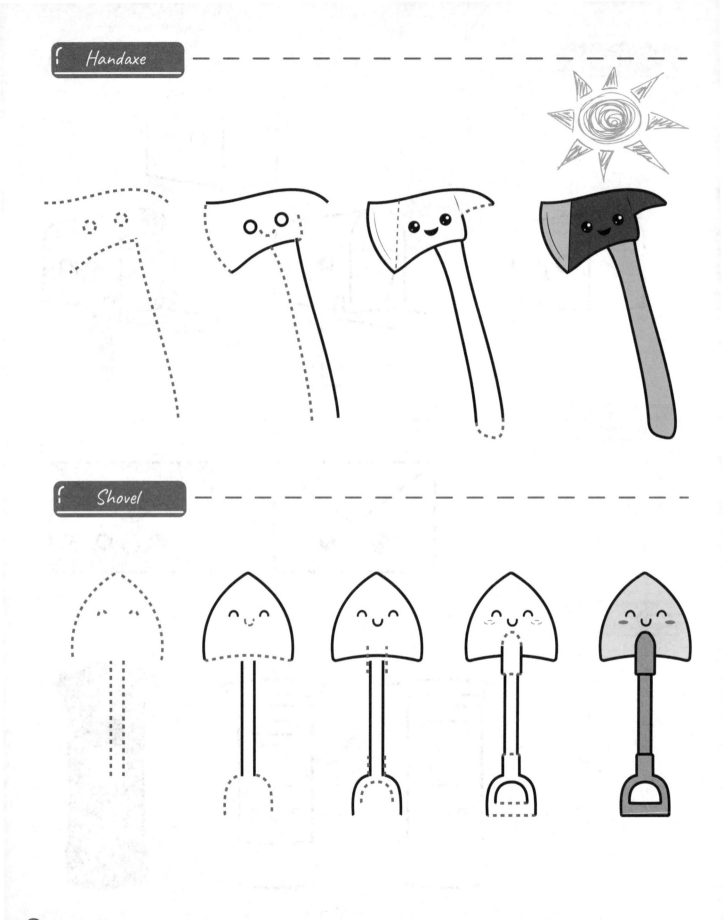

Shovel

Koi Pond

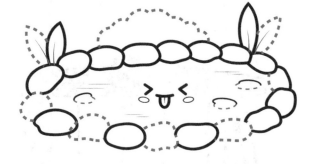

Koi Fish

Swings

Pond

Slide

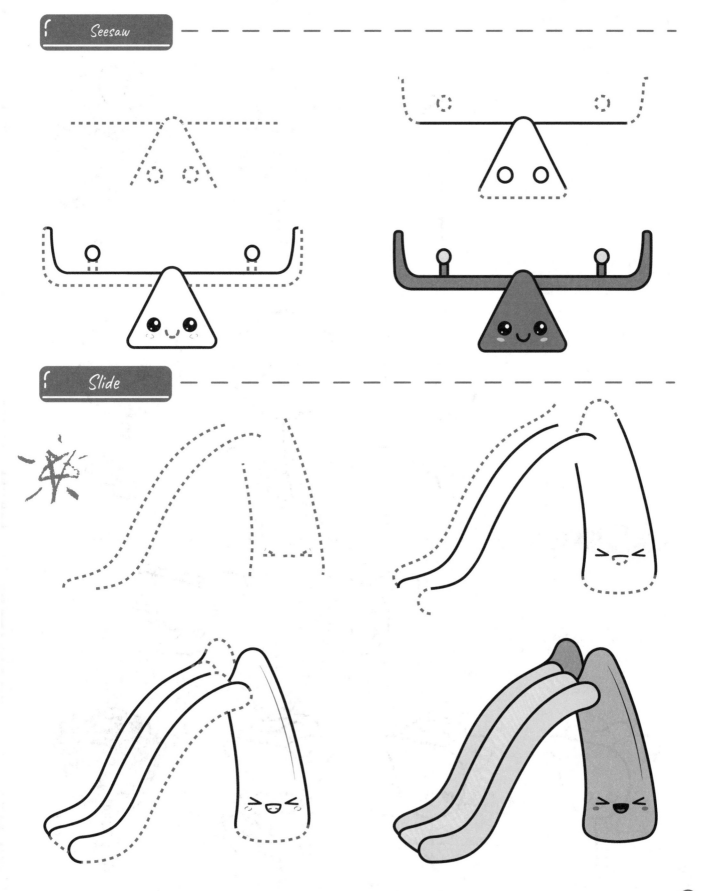

Daisy

Dandelion

Rose

Garden Boots

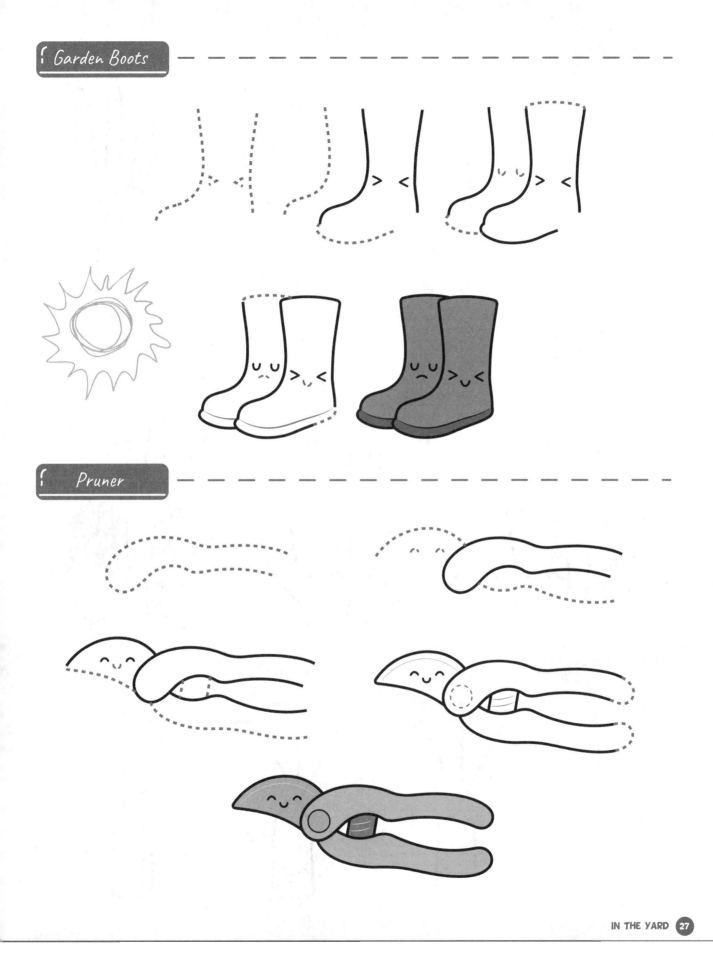

Pruner

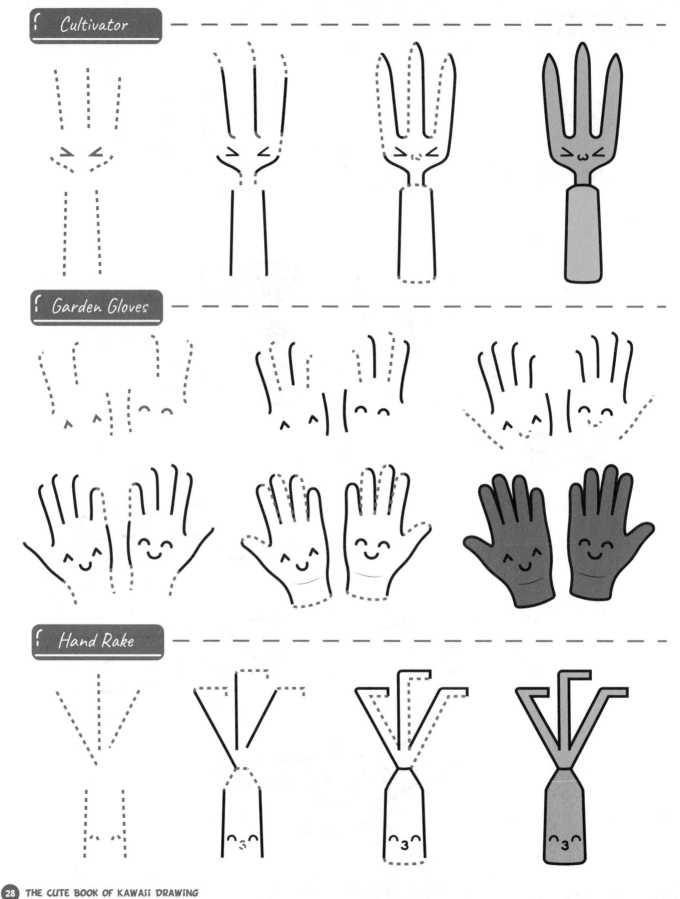

Cultivator

Garden Gloves

Hand Rake

Hose

Hand Trowel

Flower Bed

Cone

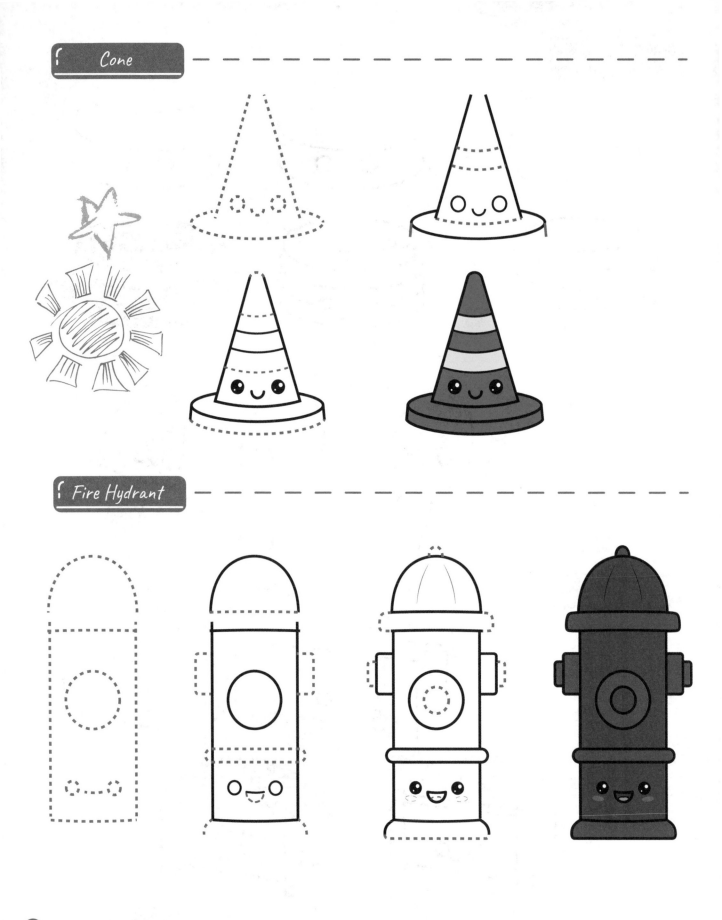

Fire Hydrant

Toucan

Owl

Bald Eagle

Raven

Flamingo

Penguin

Budgie

Duck

Chicken

Seagull

Blue Jay

Cardinal

Pigeon

Vulture

Ostrich

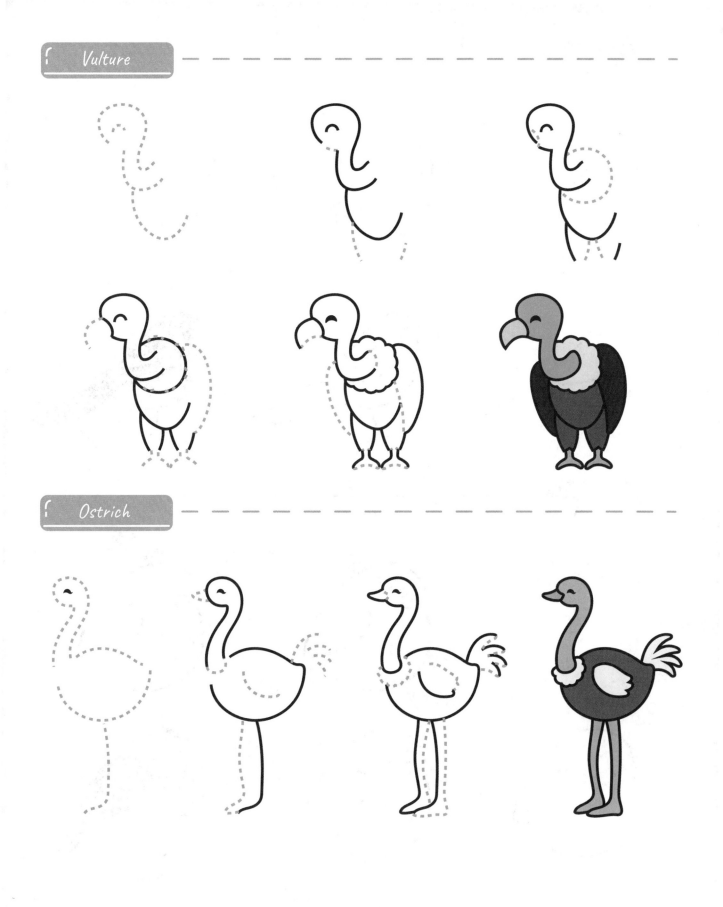

Magpie

Robin

Airplane

Small Plane

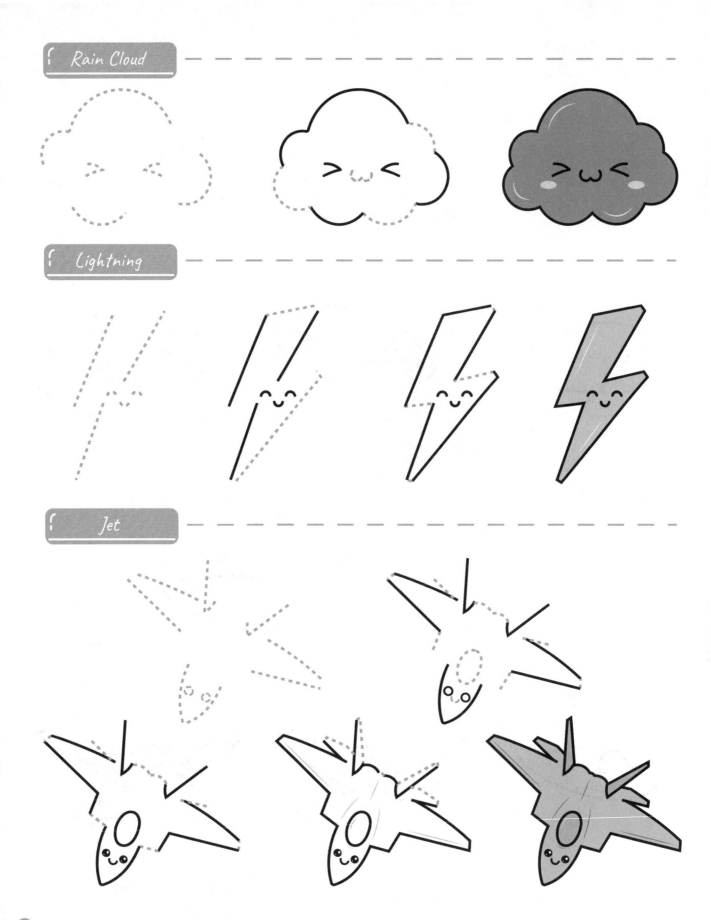

Rain Cloud

Lightning

Jet

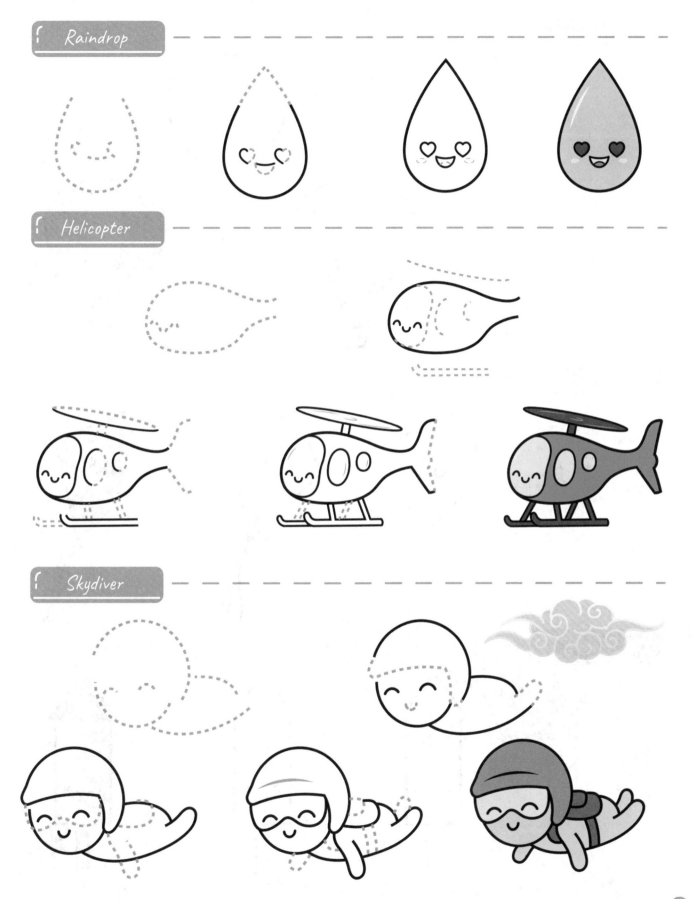

Raindrop

Helicopter

Skydiver

Hot Air Balloon

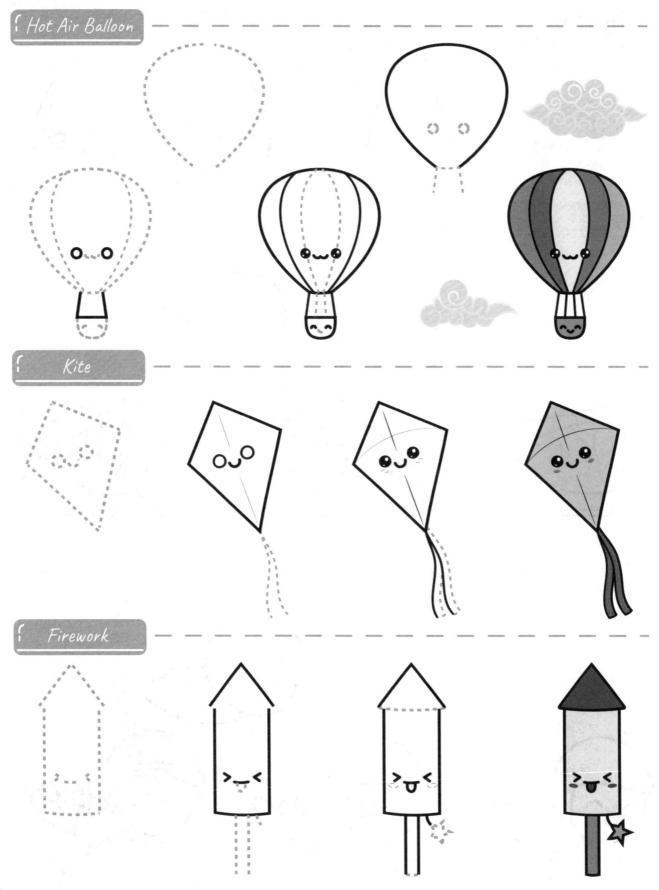

Kite

Firework

SPACE & DINOS

Astronaut

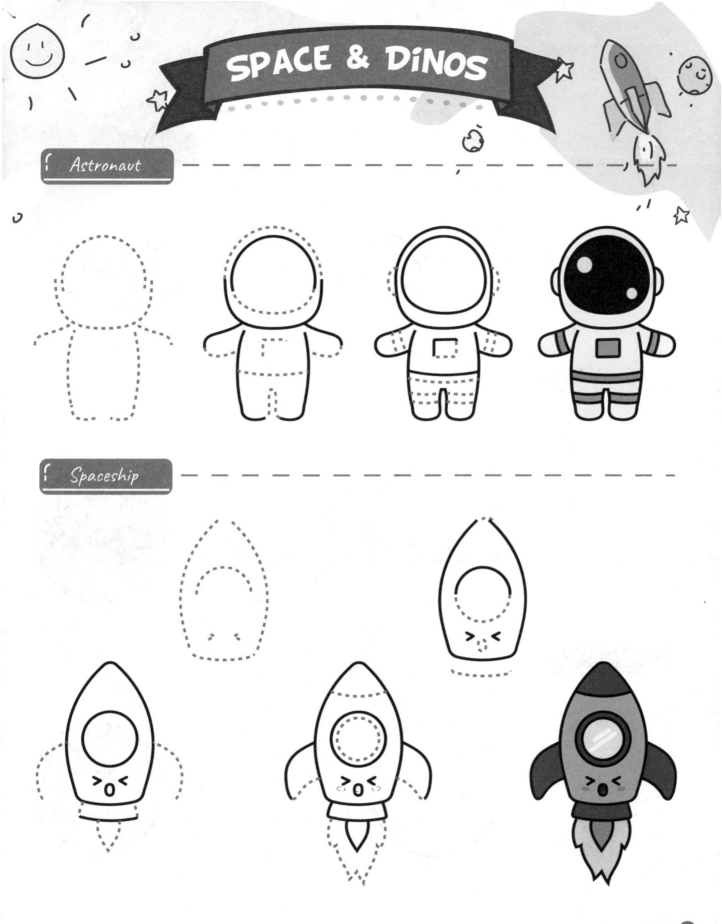

Spaceship

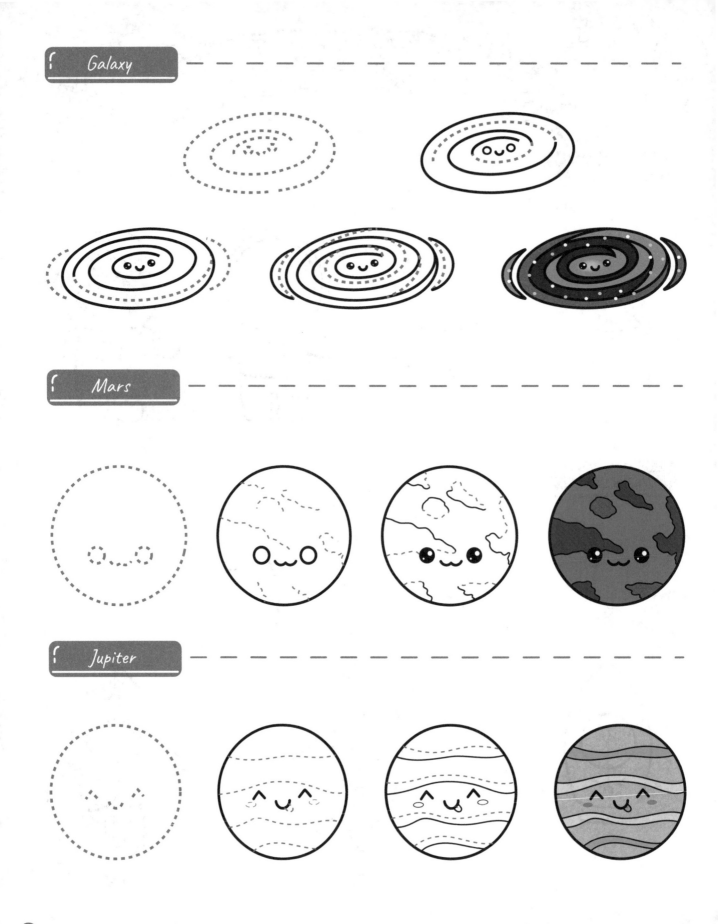

Galaxy

Mars

Jupiter

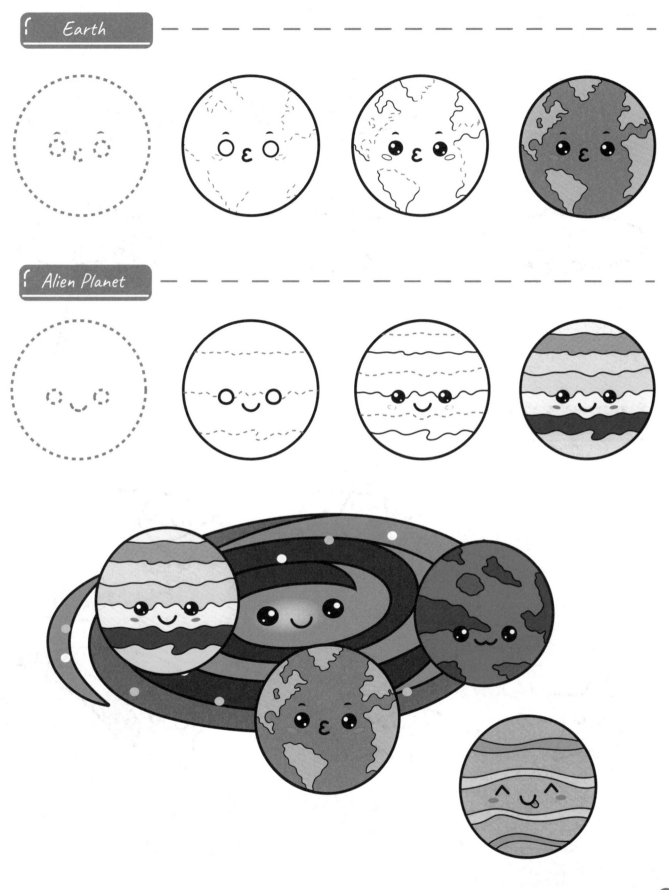

Earth

Alien Planet

U.F.O.

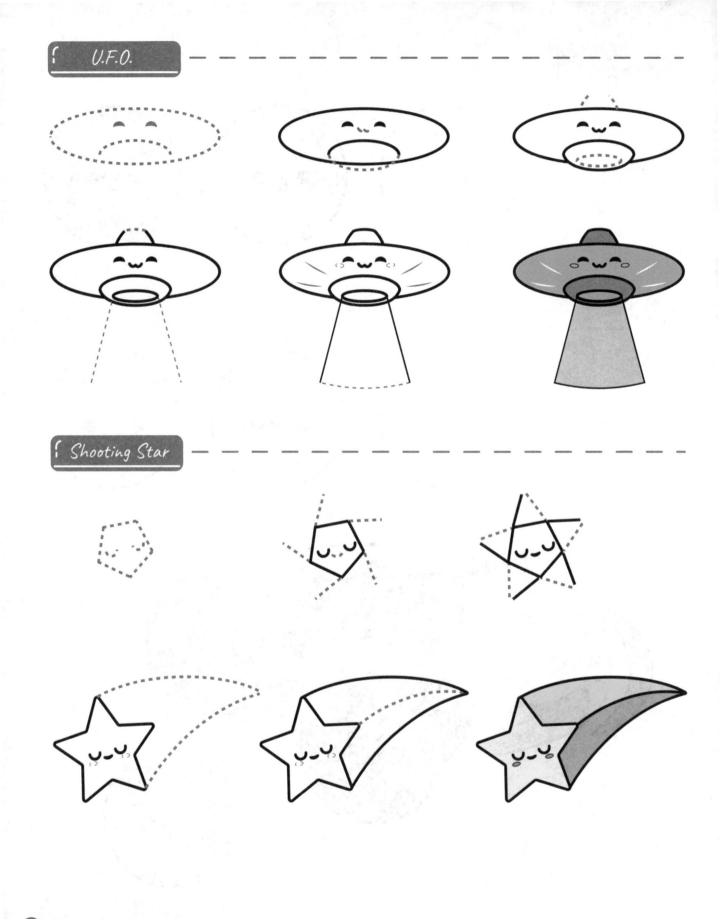

Shooting Star

Moon

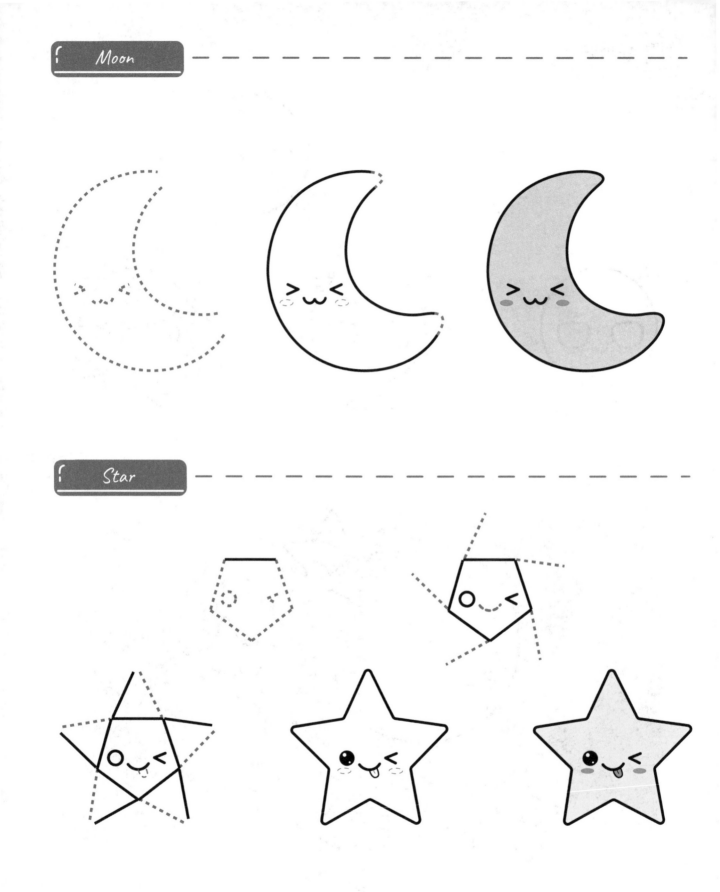

Star

Allosaurus

Dilophosaurus

Kentrosaurus

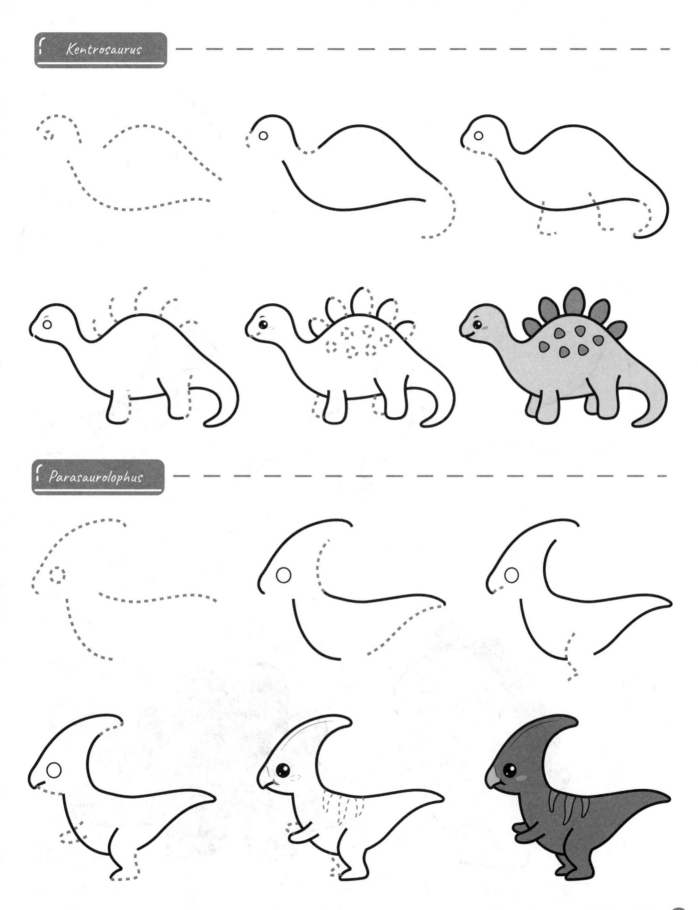

Parasaurolophus

Dacentrurus

Stegosaurus

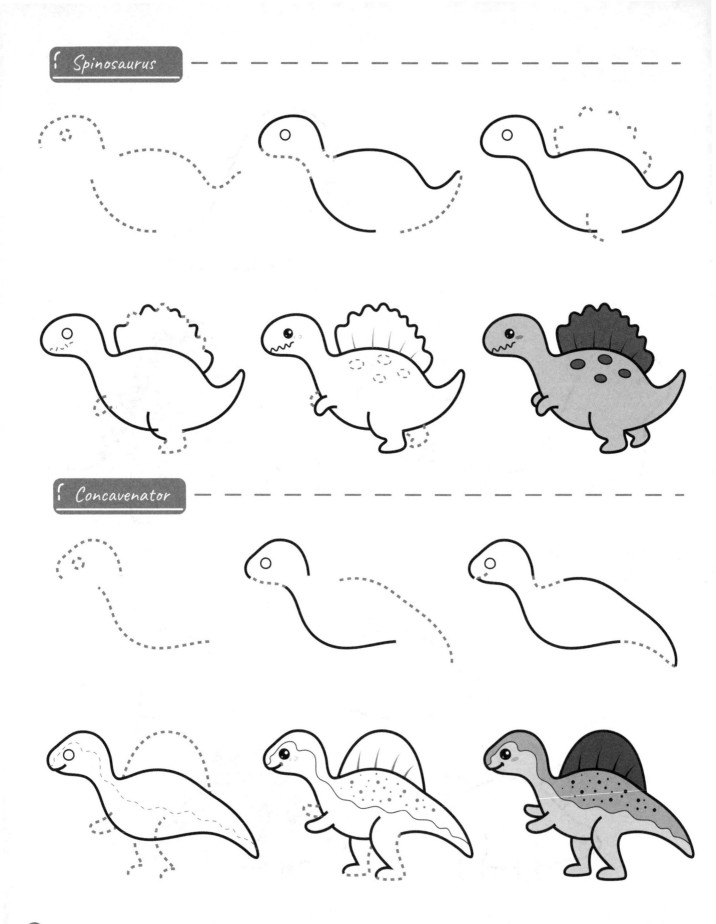

Spinosaurus

Concavenator

IN THE WATER

Walrus

Goldfish

Betta Fish

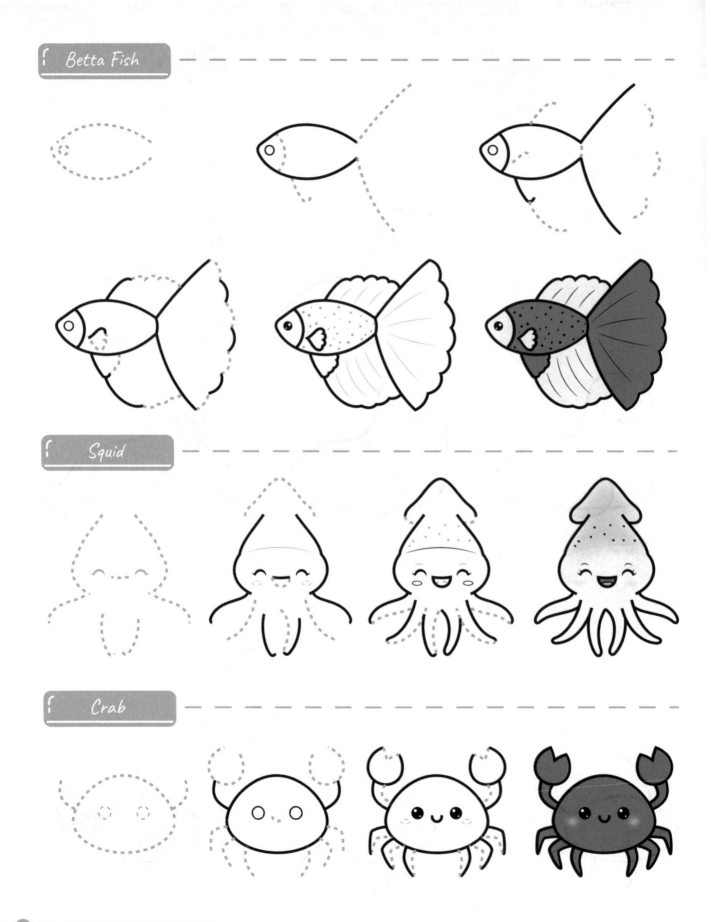

Squid

Crab

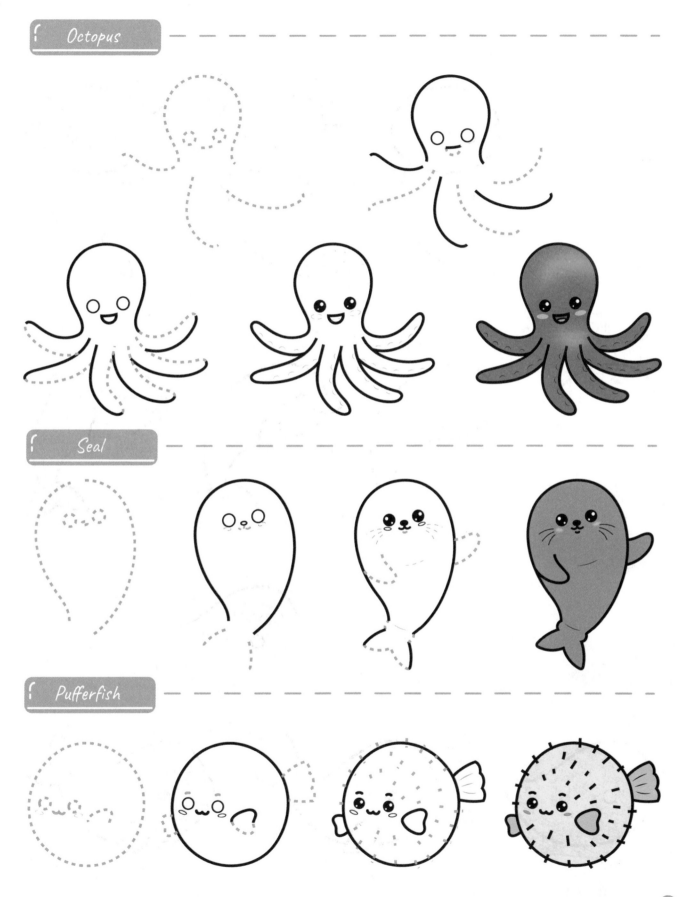

Octopus

Seal

Pufferfish

Axolotl

Dolphin

Whale

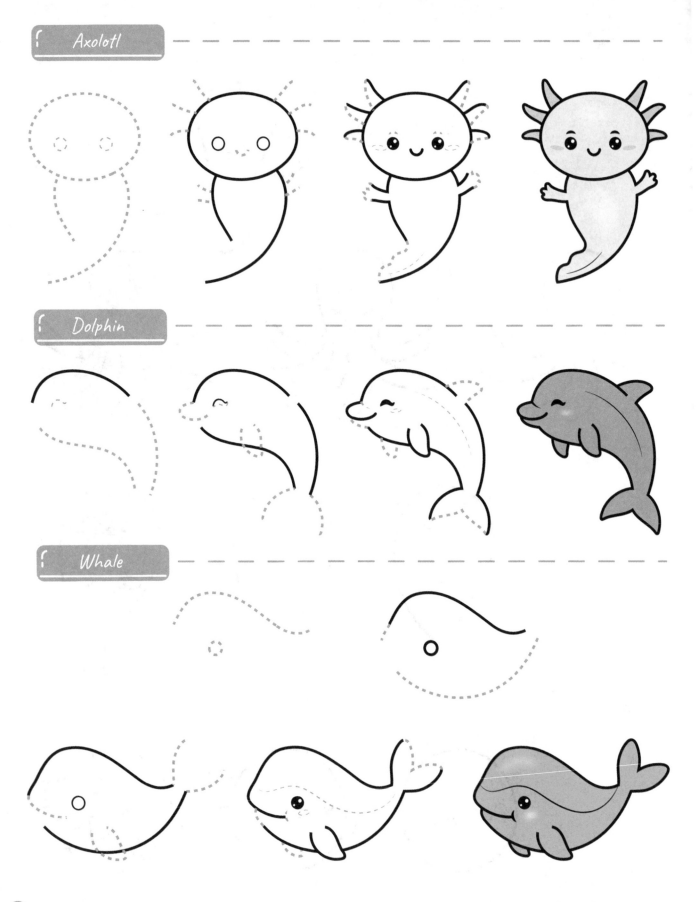

Purple Queen

Angelfish

Sea Turtle

Shark

Swordfish

Blue Tang

Tropical Fish

Seahorse

Starfish

Happy Fish

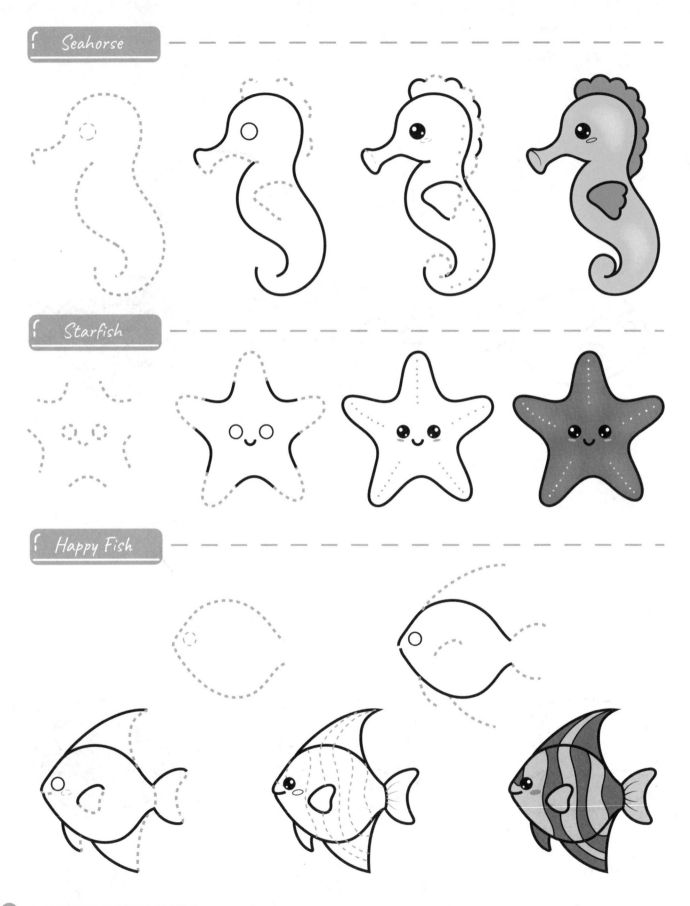

Queen Parrotfish

Tugboat

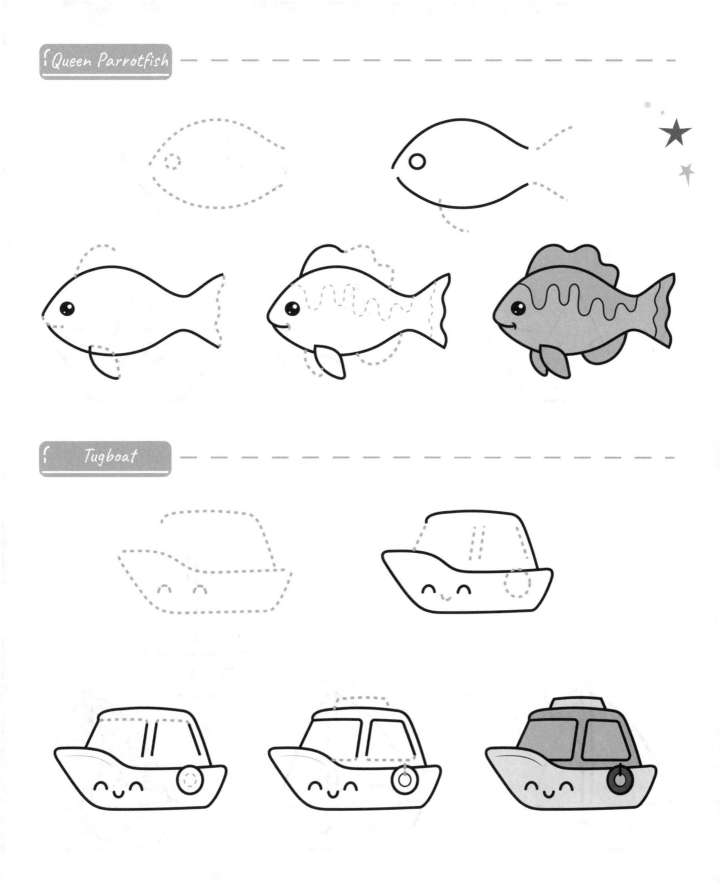

Paper Boat

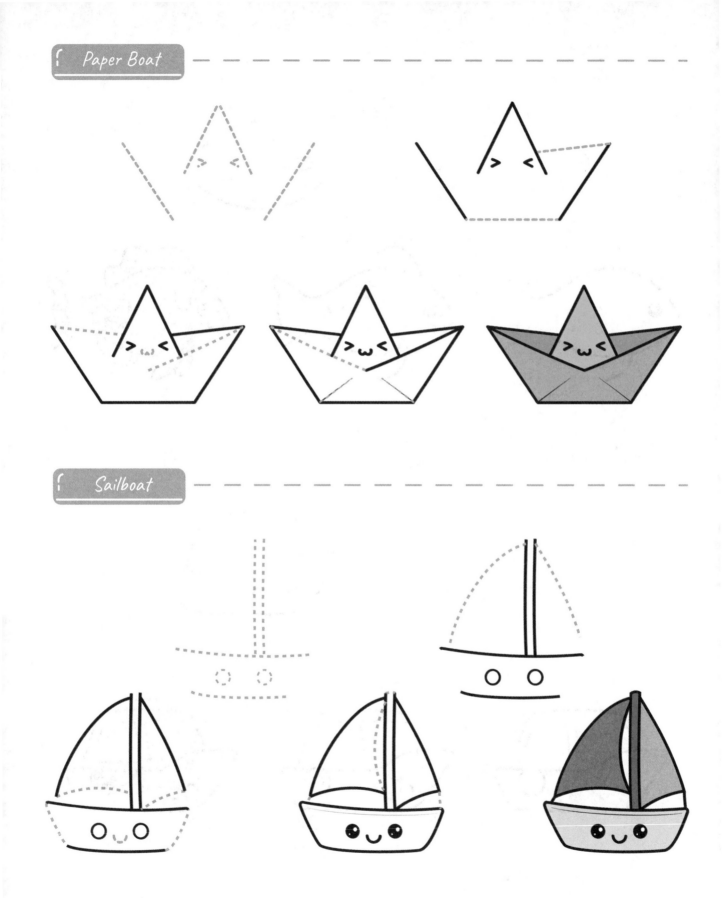

Sailboat

Toilet Paper

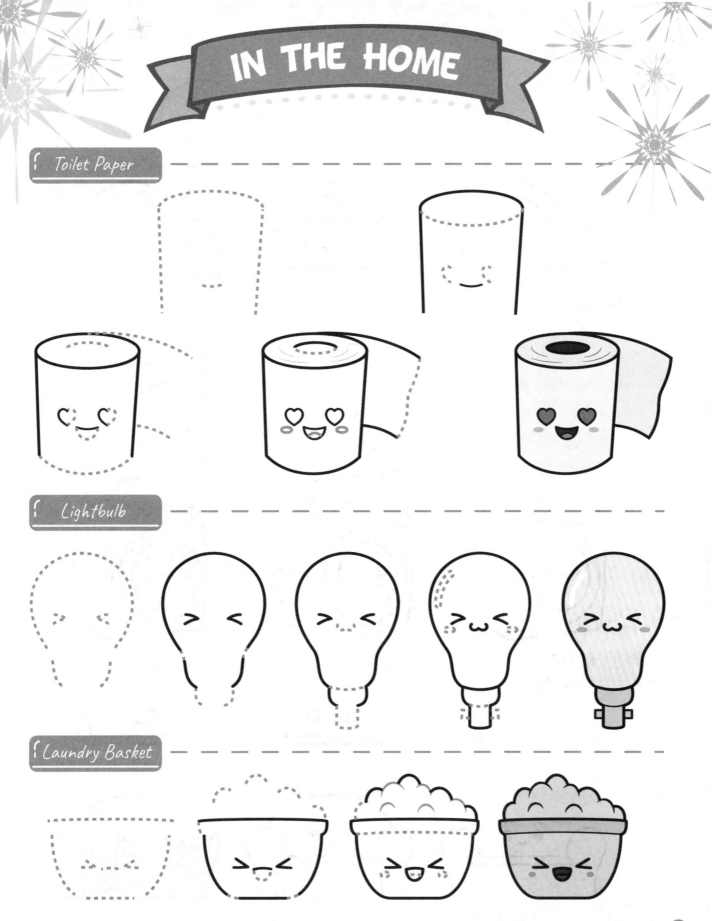

Lightbulb

Laundry Basket

Clothes Iron

Laundry Machine

Couch

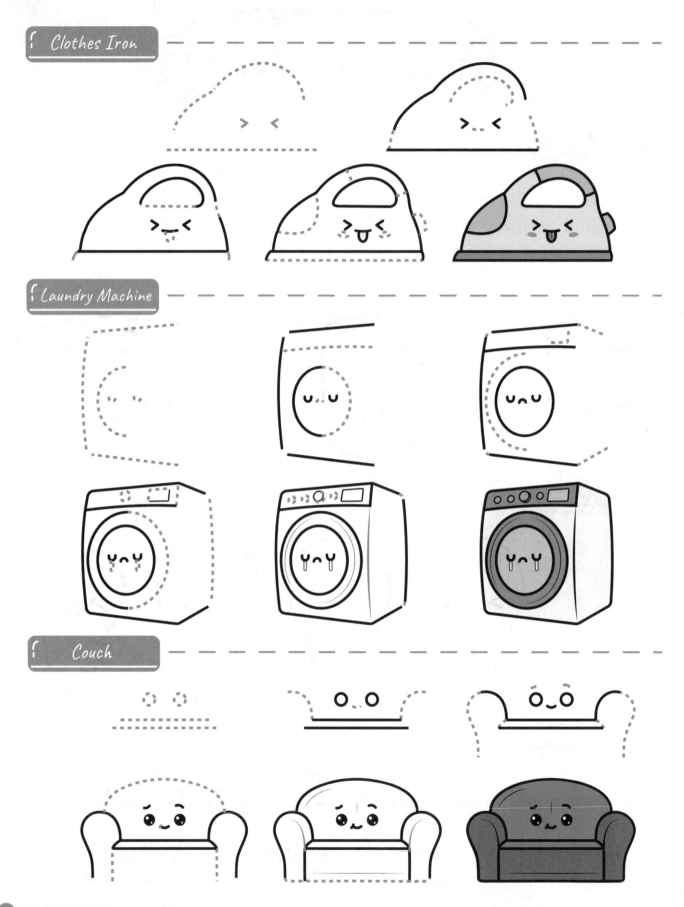

Dustpan

Soap

Trash Can

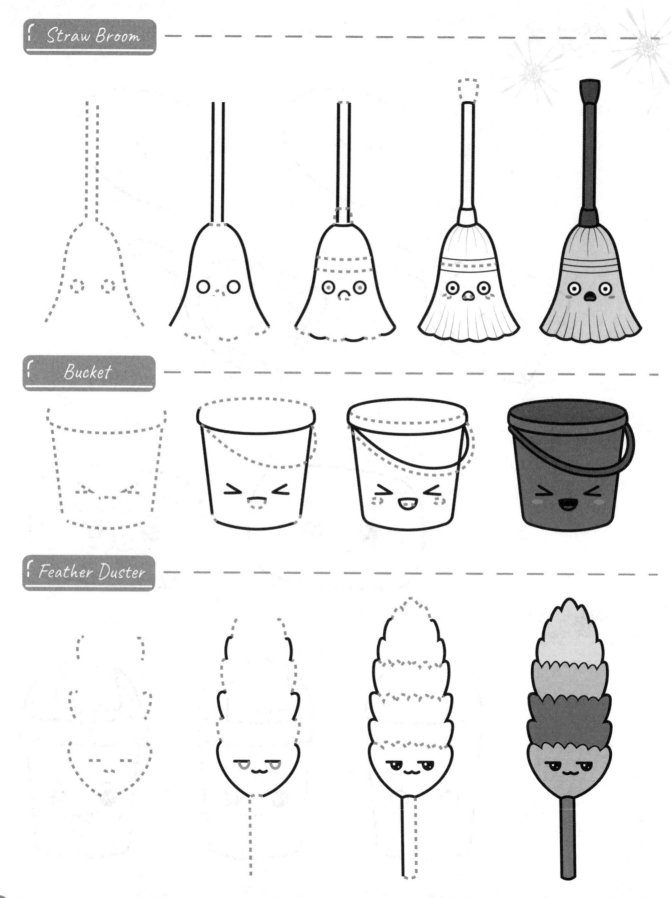

Straw Broom

Bucket

Feather Duster

Cleaning Broom

Sponge

Spray Bottle

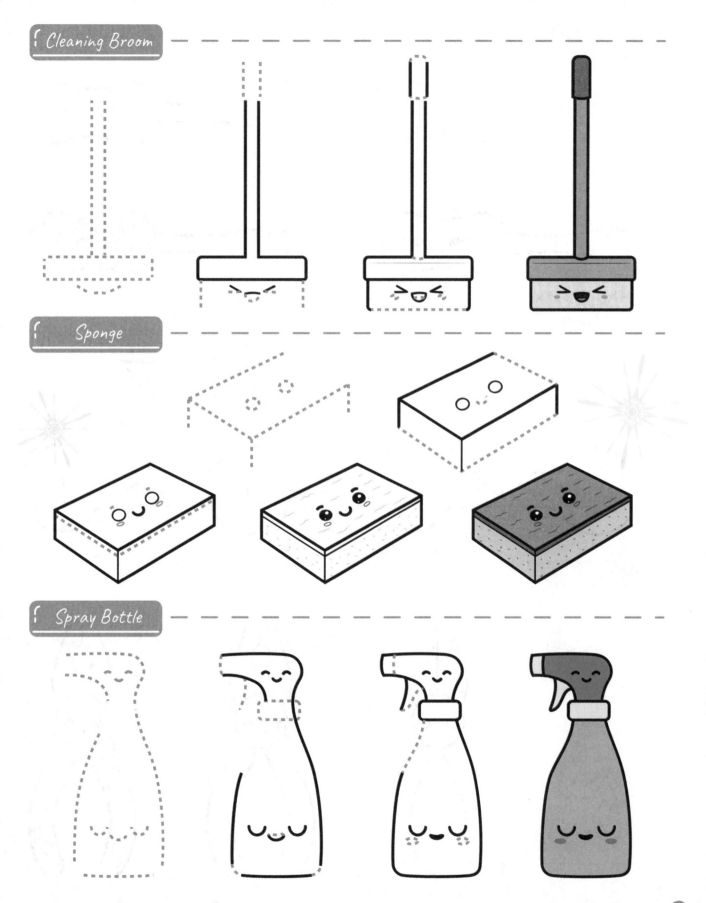

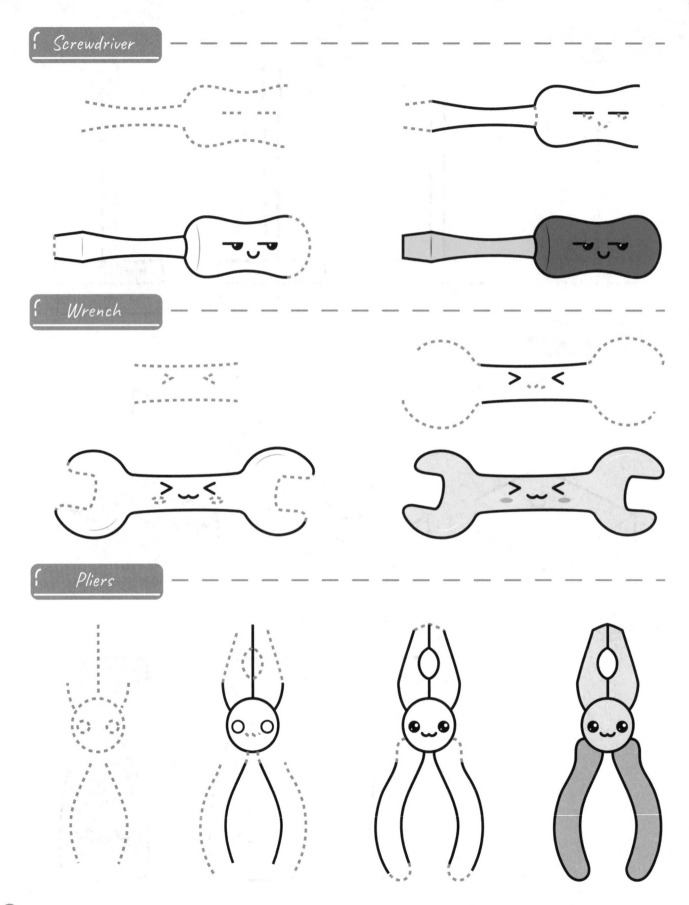

Screwdriver

Wrench

Pliers

Cardboard Box

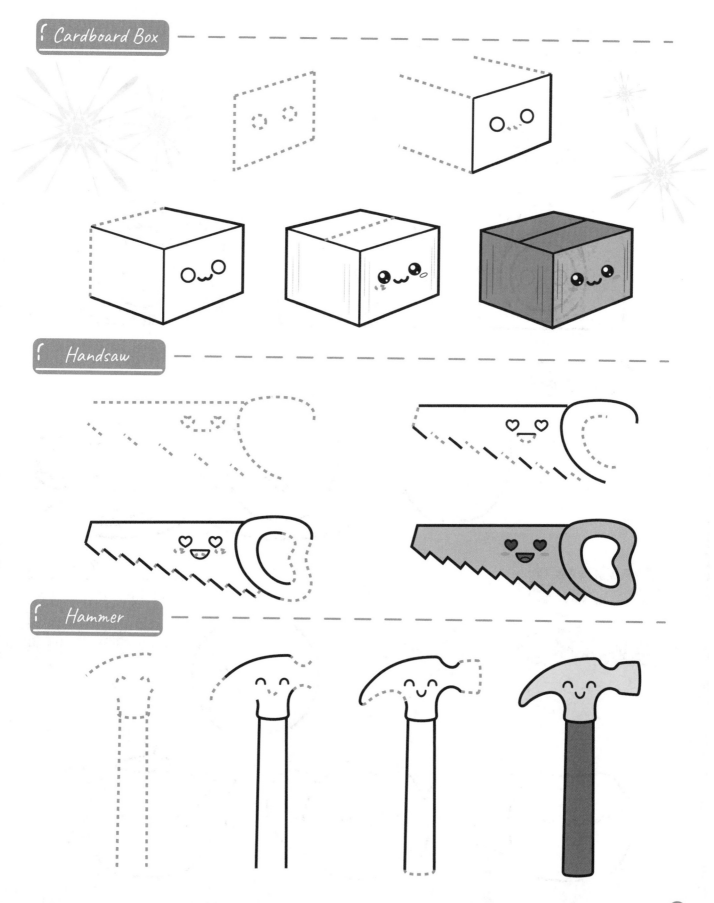

Handsaw

Hammer

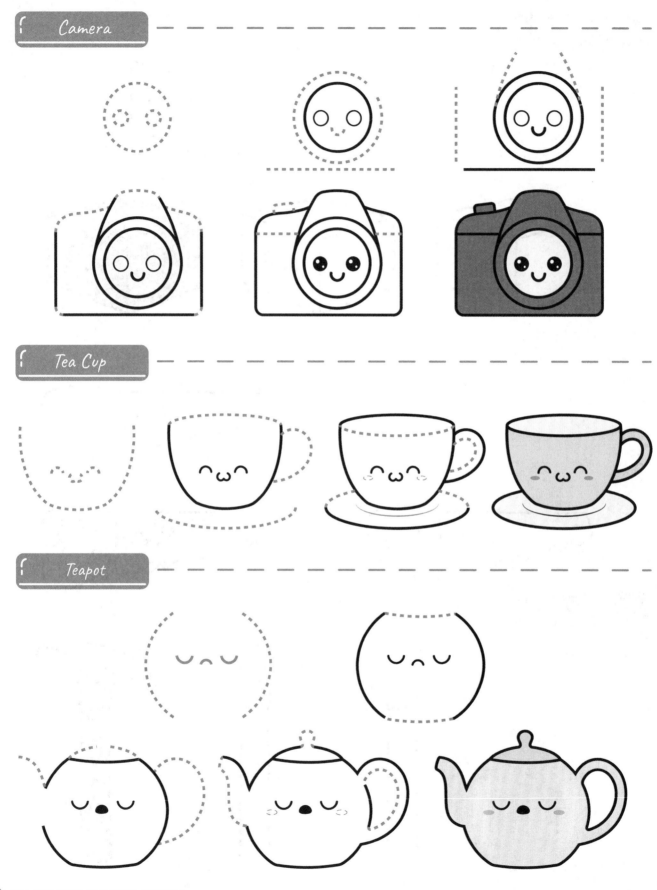

Camera

Tea Cup

Teapot

Radio

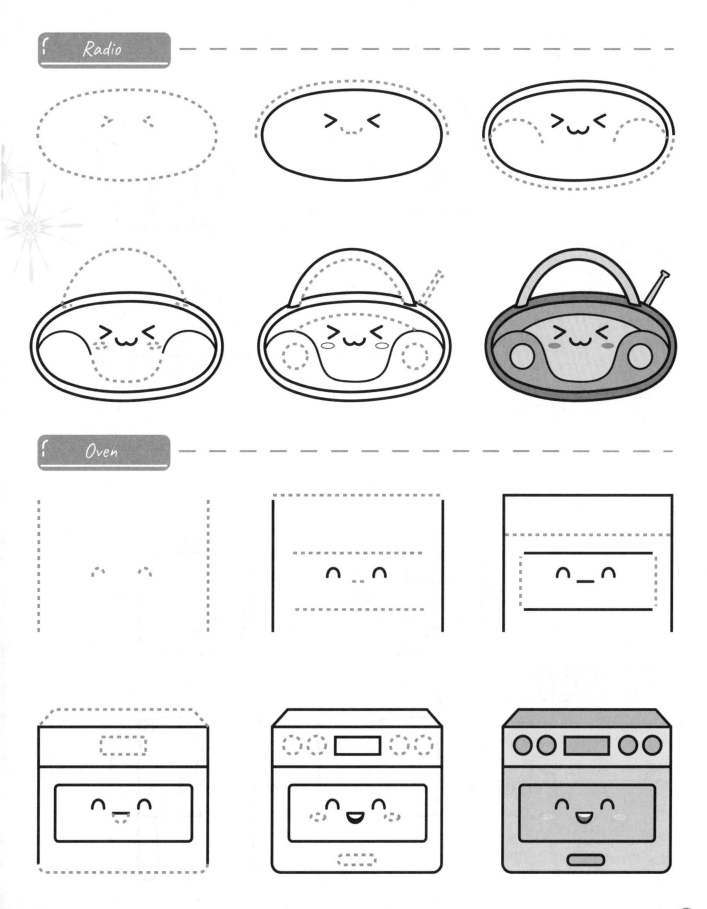

Oven

Oven Mitt

Serving Tray

Cooking Pot

Butcher's Knife

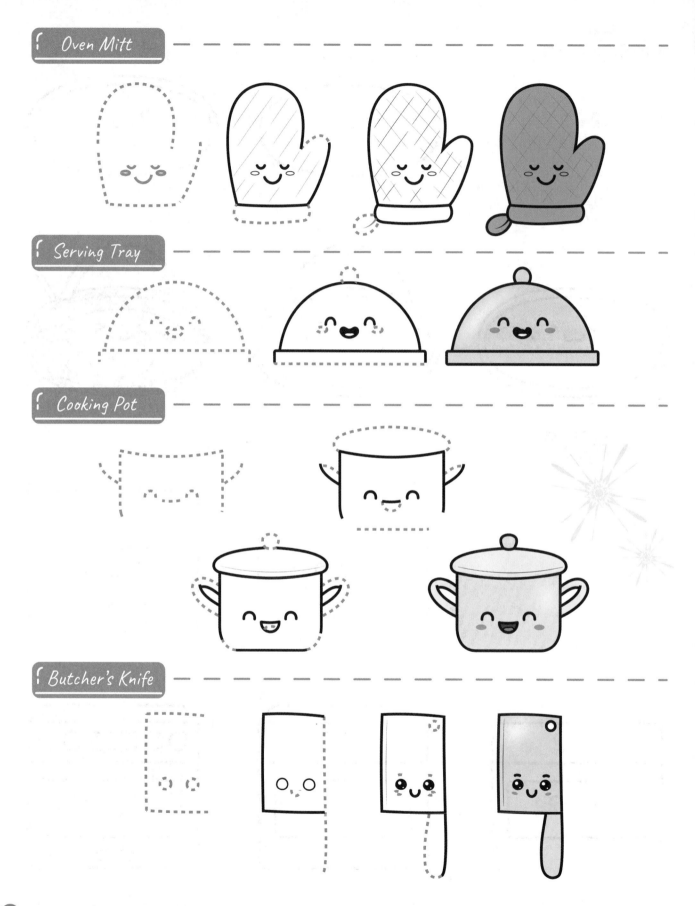

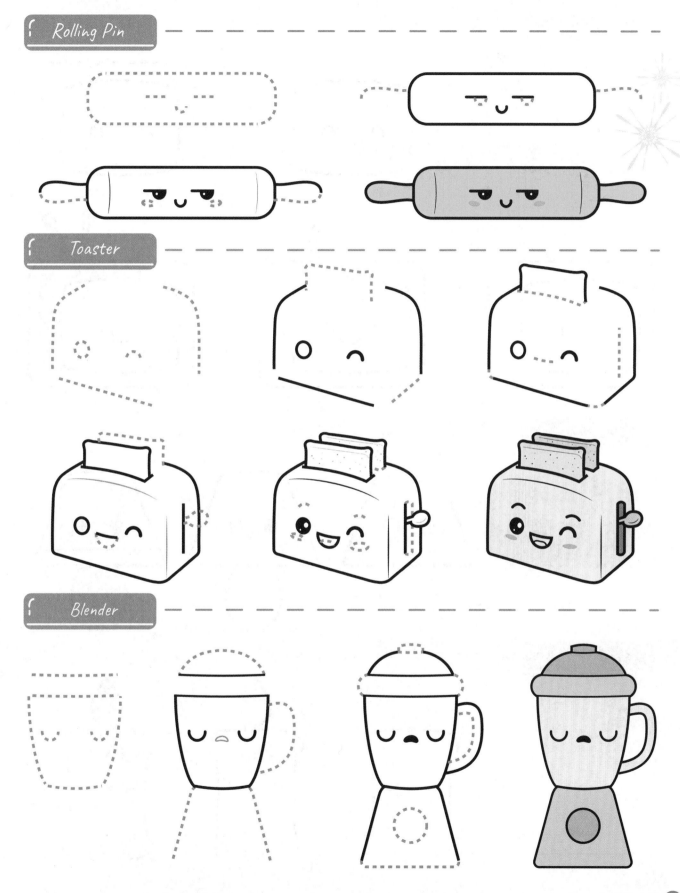

Rolling Pin

Toaster

Blender

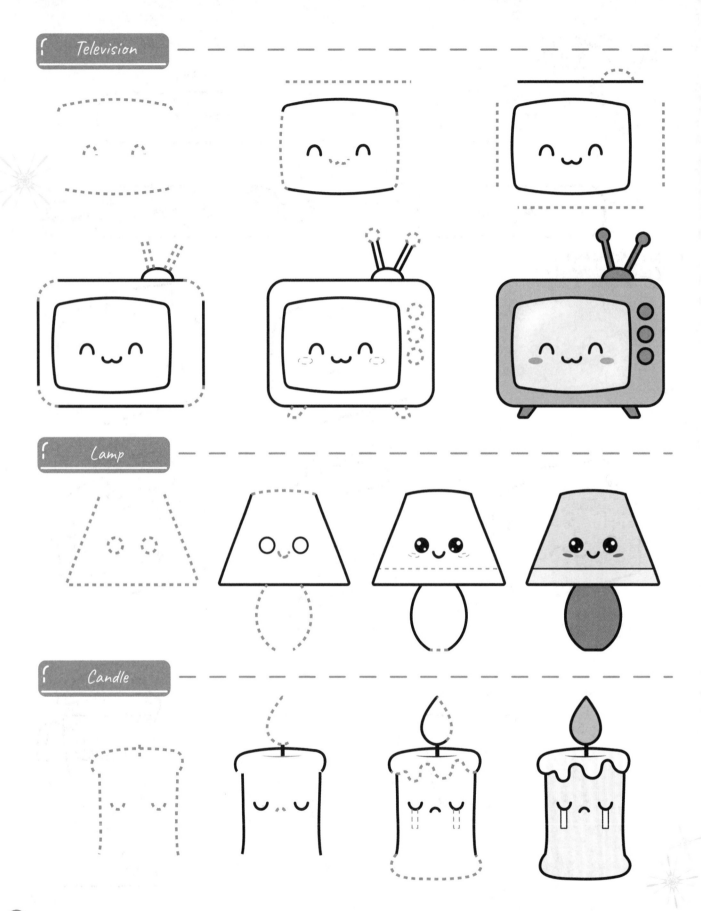

Television

Lamp

Candle

CUTE PEOPLE & THINGS

Teacher

Schoolbus

Backpack

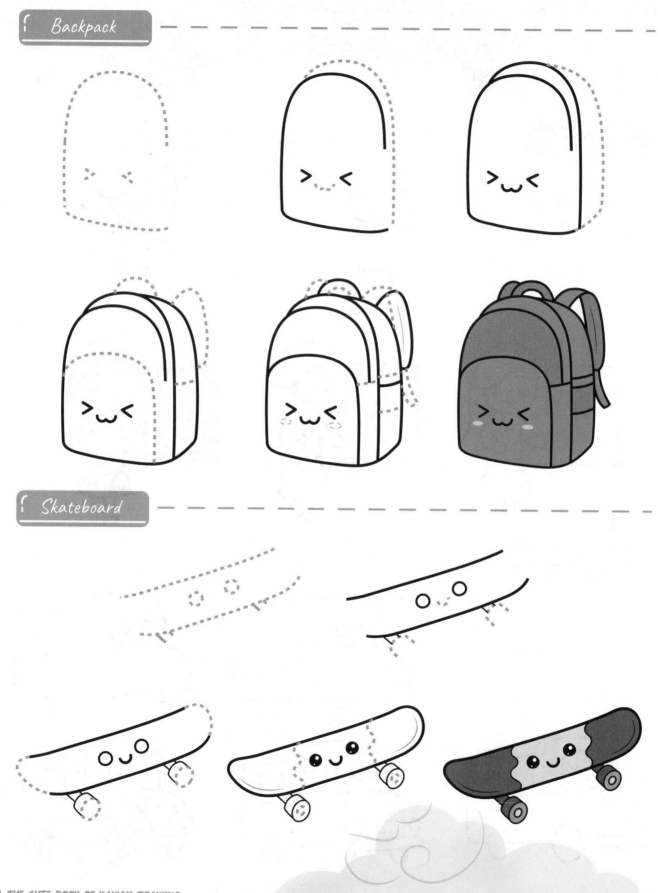

Skateboard

Ethan

Siobhan

Joaquin

Nurse

Sam

Helga

Michael

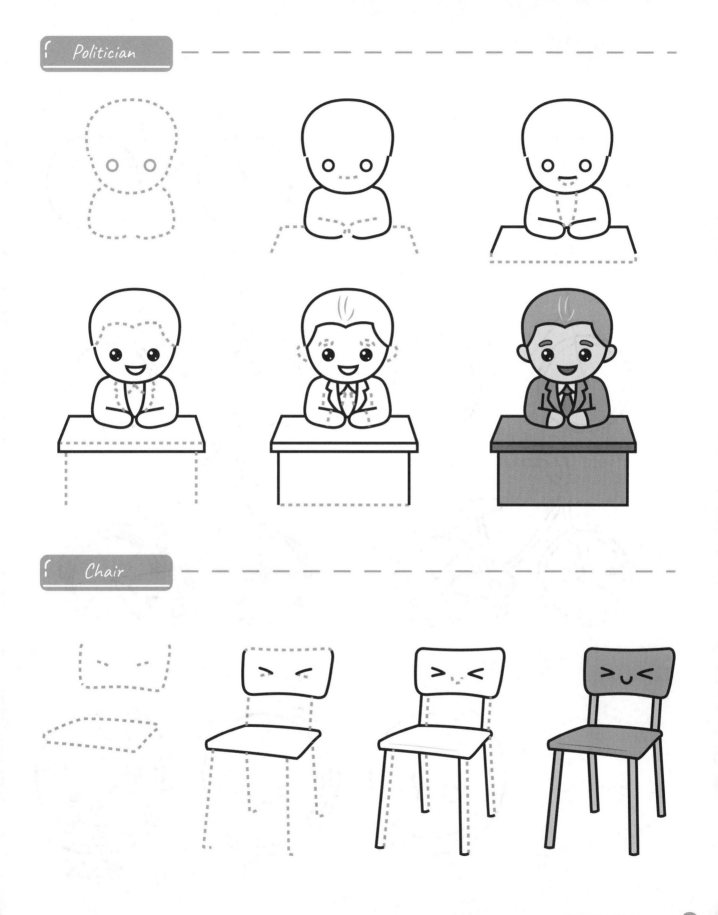

Chair

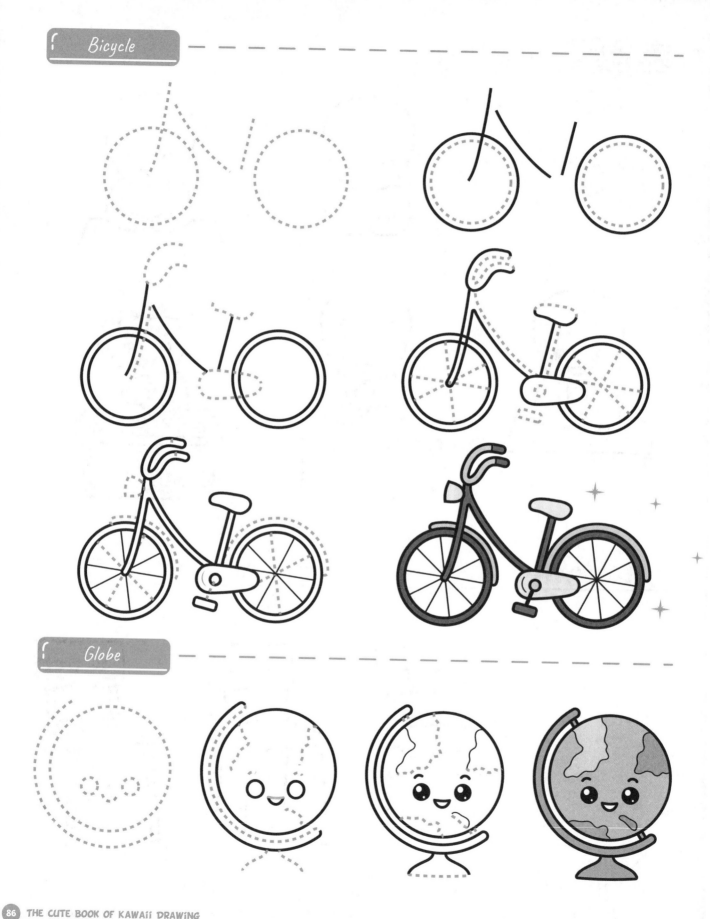

Bicycle

Globe

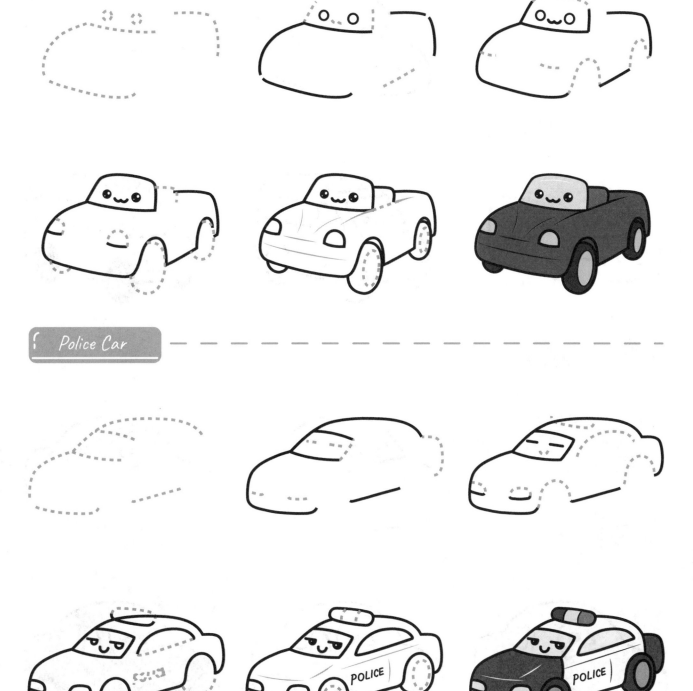

Police Car

Ambulance

Sedan

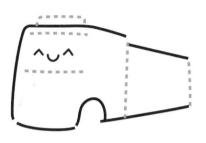

Van

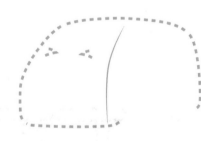

Hourglass

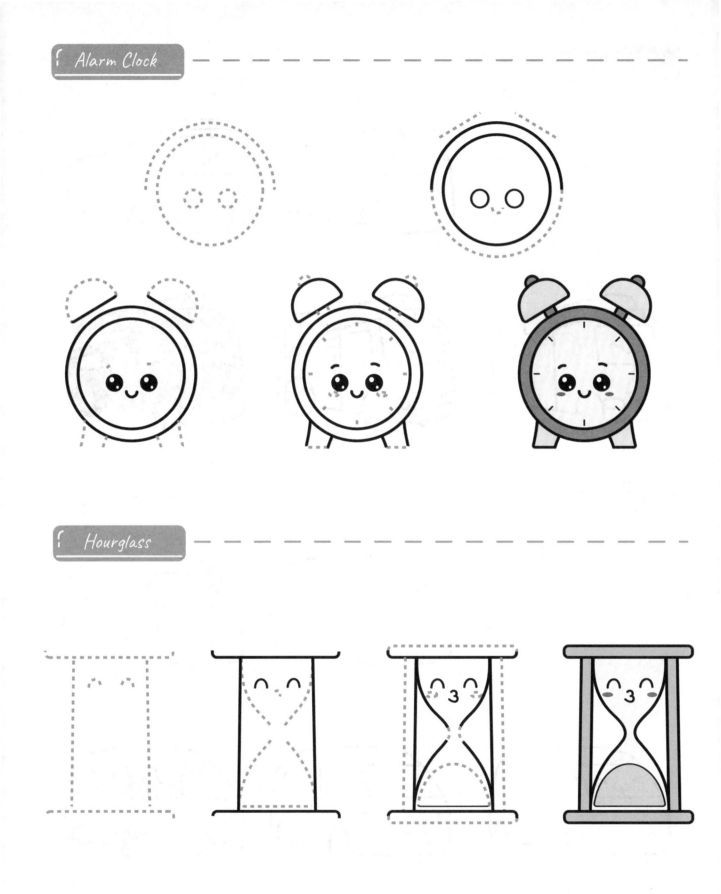

Water Bottle

Wristwatch

Diamond

Baseball Cap

Cowboy Hat

Pretty Bow

Sun Hat

Purse

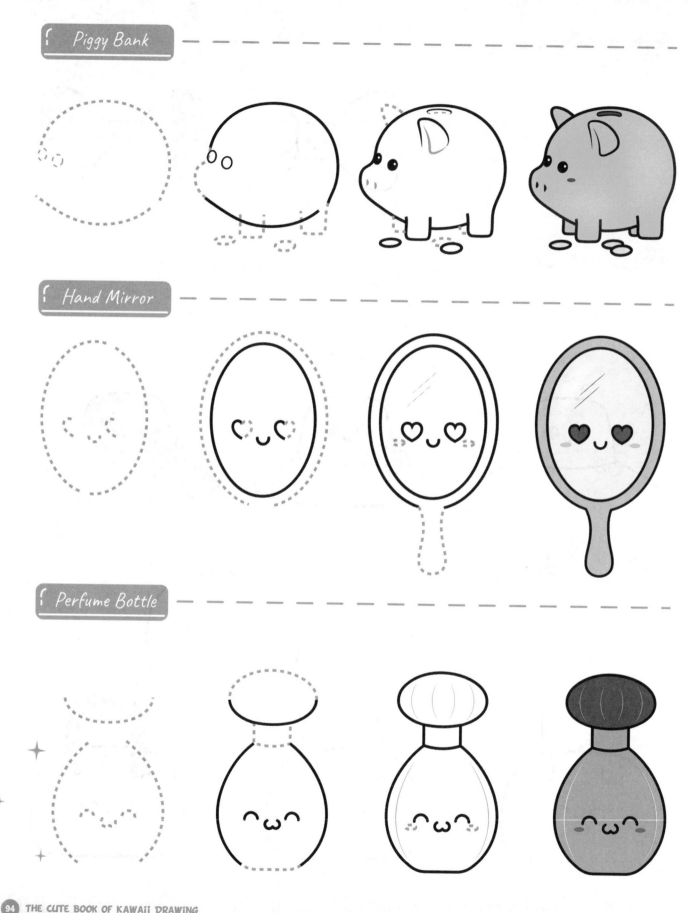

HOBBIES

Maracas

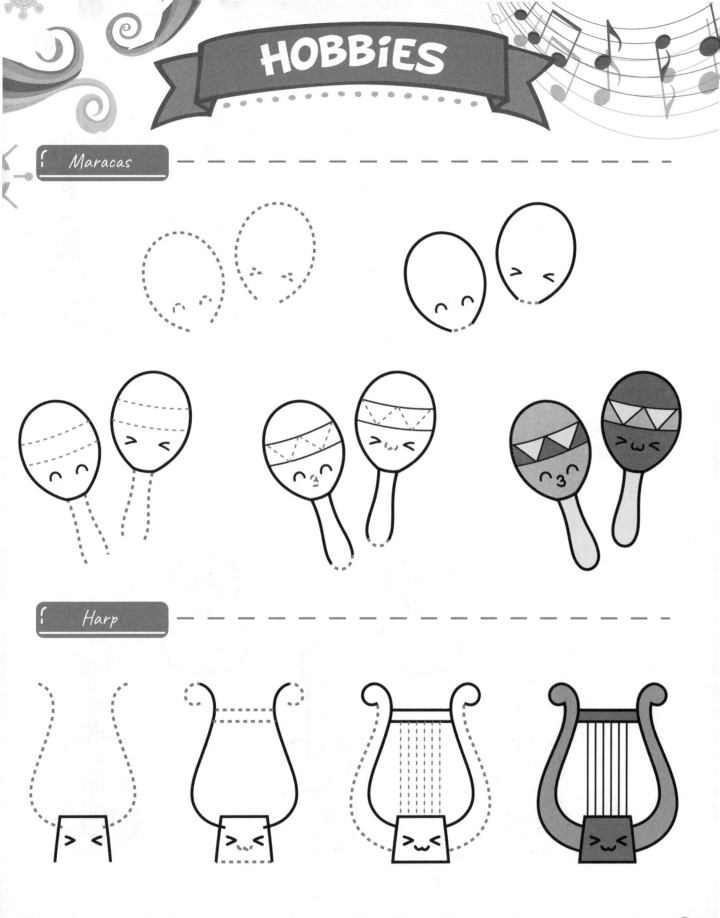

Harp

Violin

Guitar

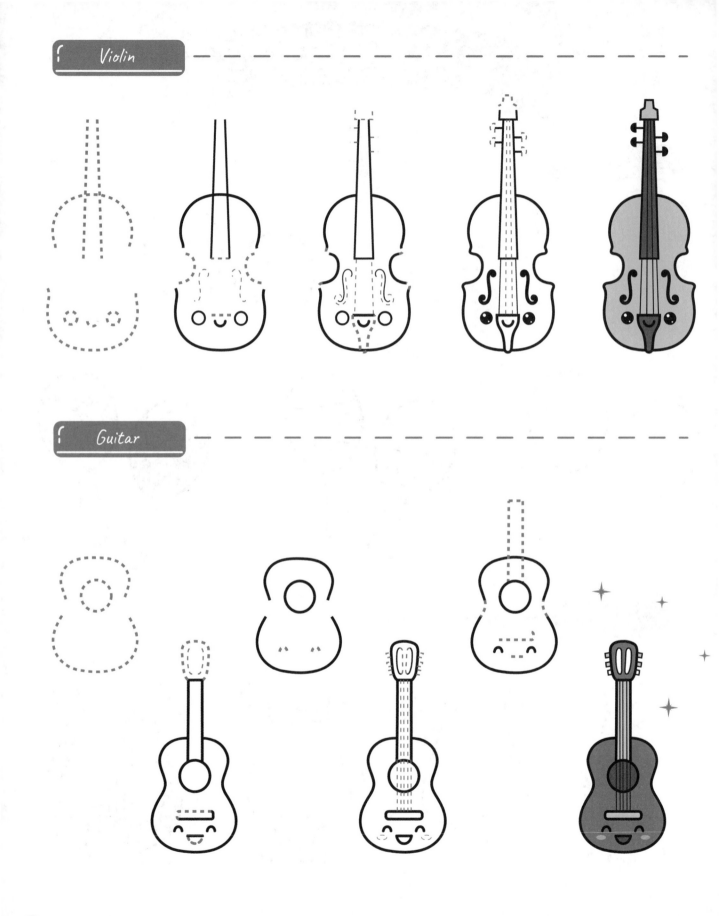

Record Player

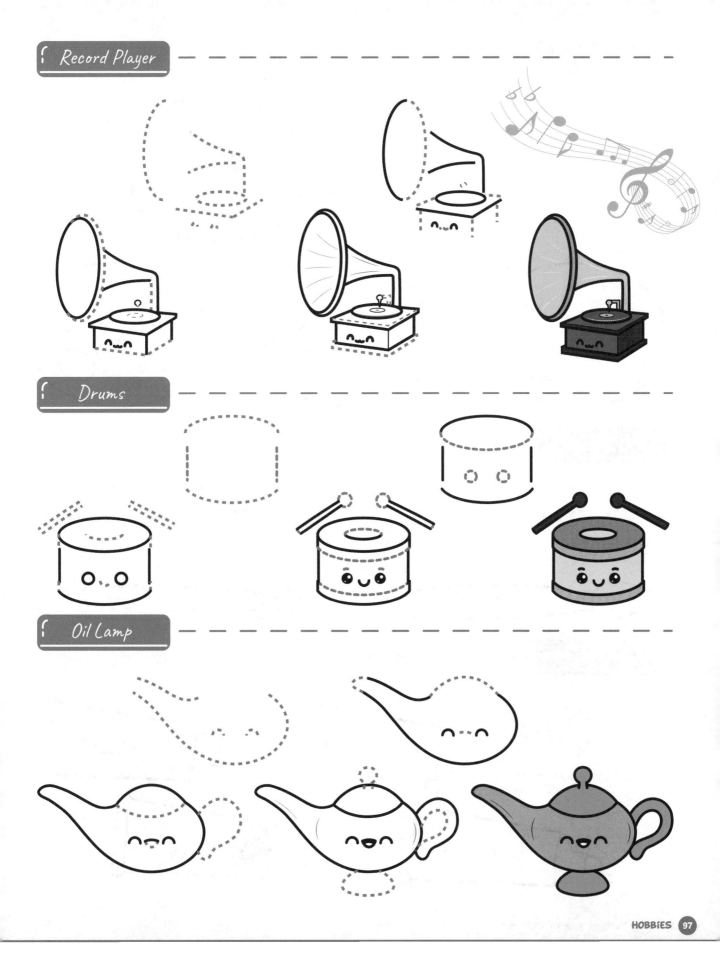

Drums

Oil Lamp

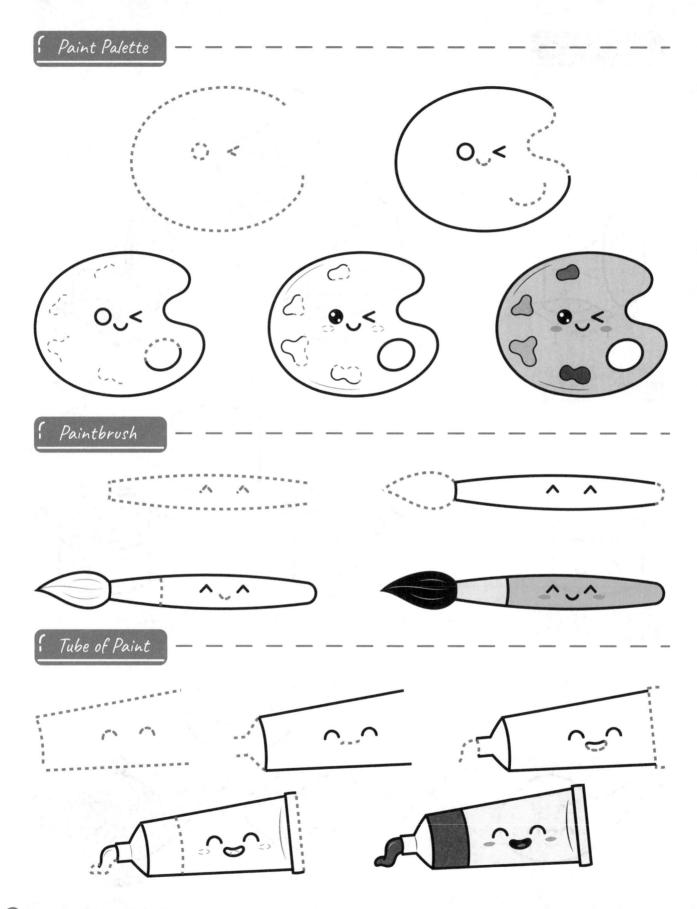

Paint Palette

Paintbrush

Tube of Paint

Big Brush

Umbrella

Crayon

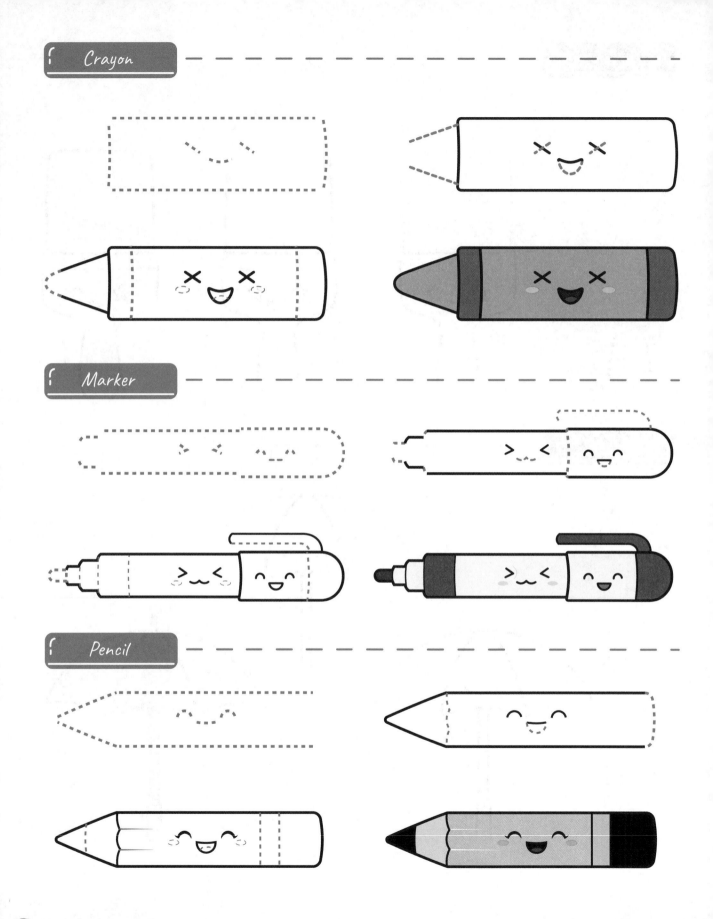

Marker

Pencil

Pen

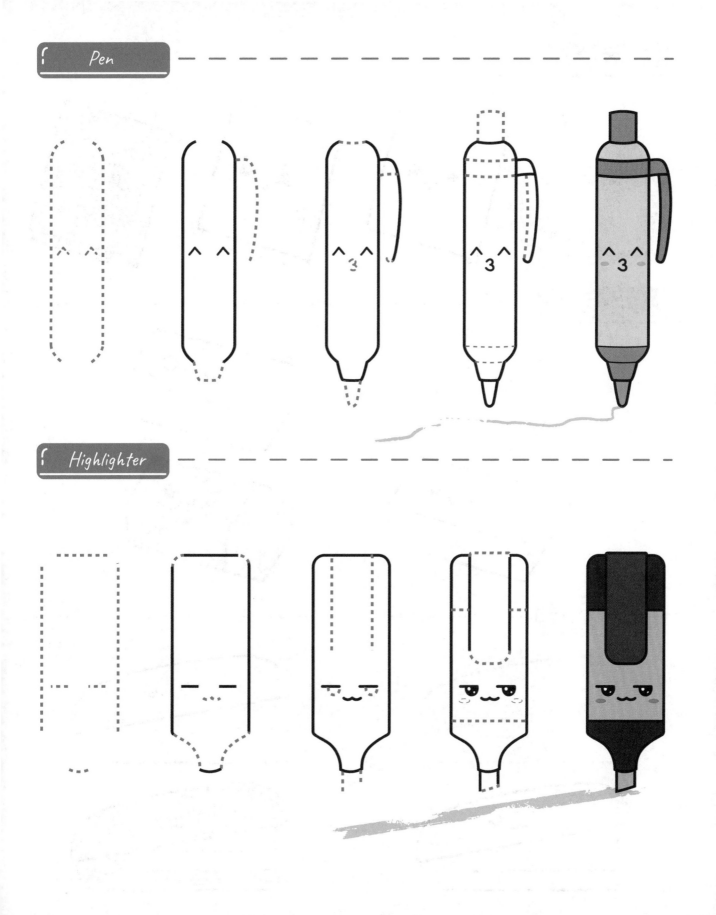

Highlighter

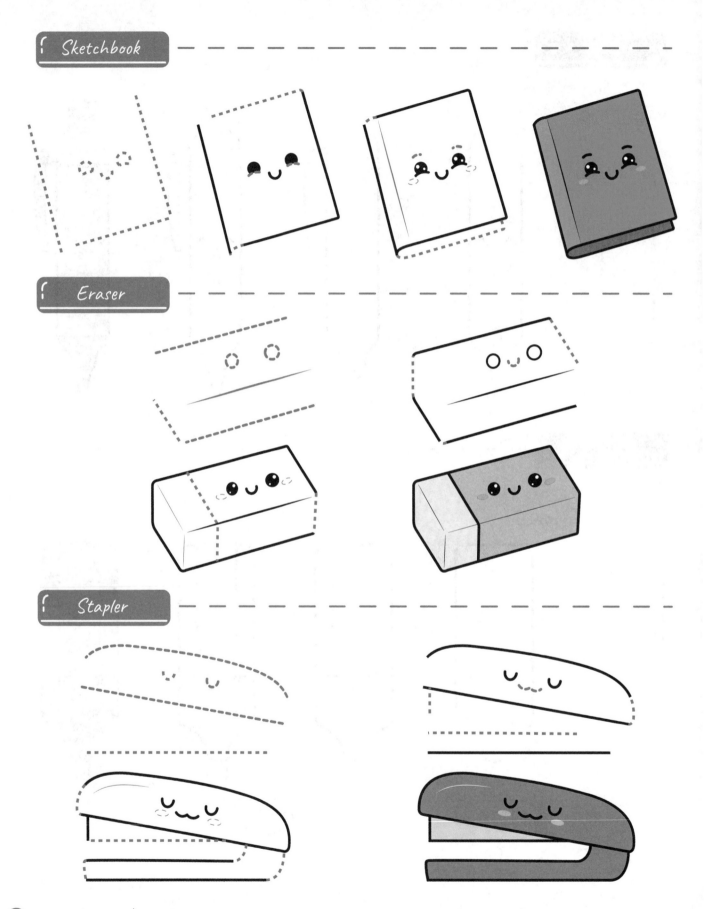

Sketchbook

Eraser

Stapler

Ruler

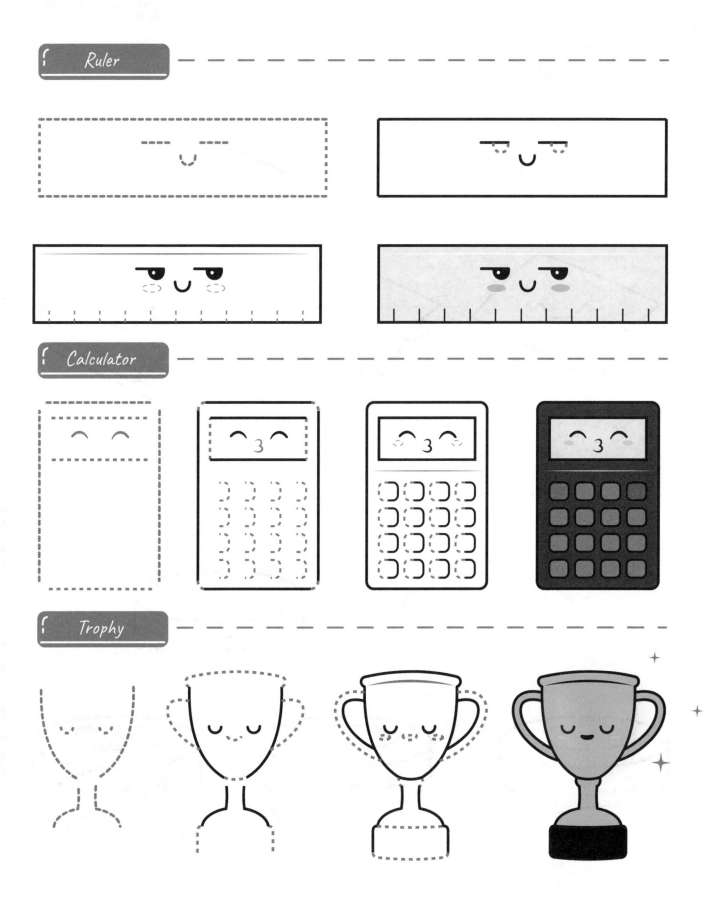

Calculator

Trophy

Roll of Tape

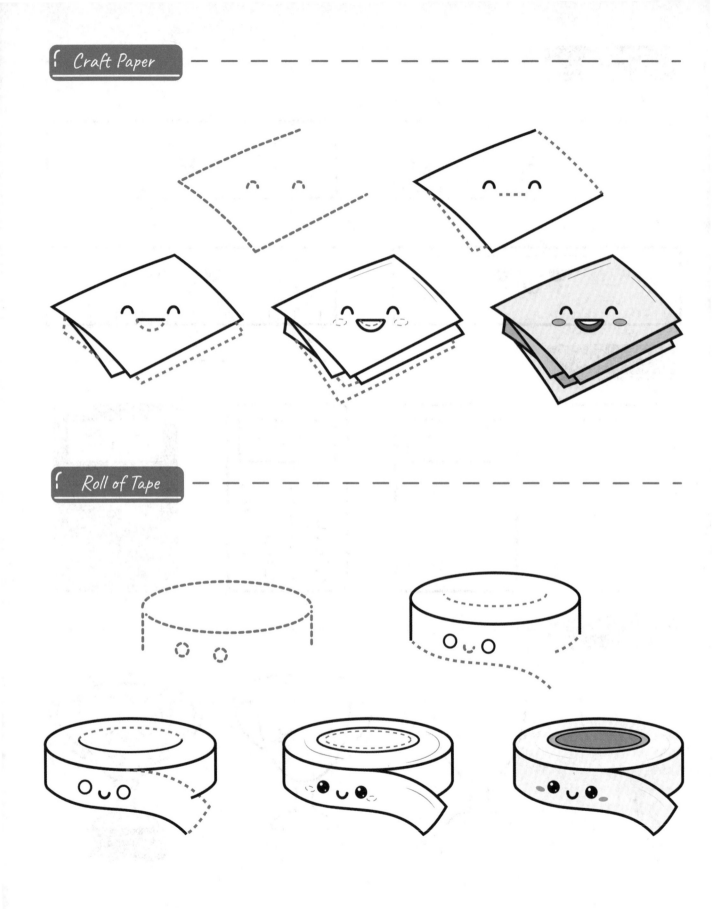

Scissors

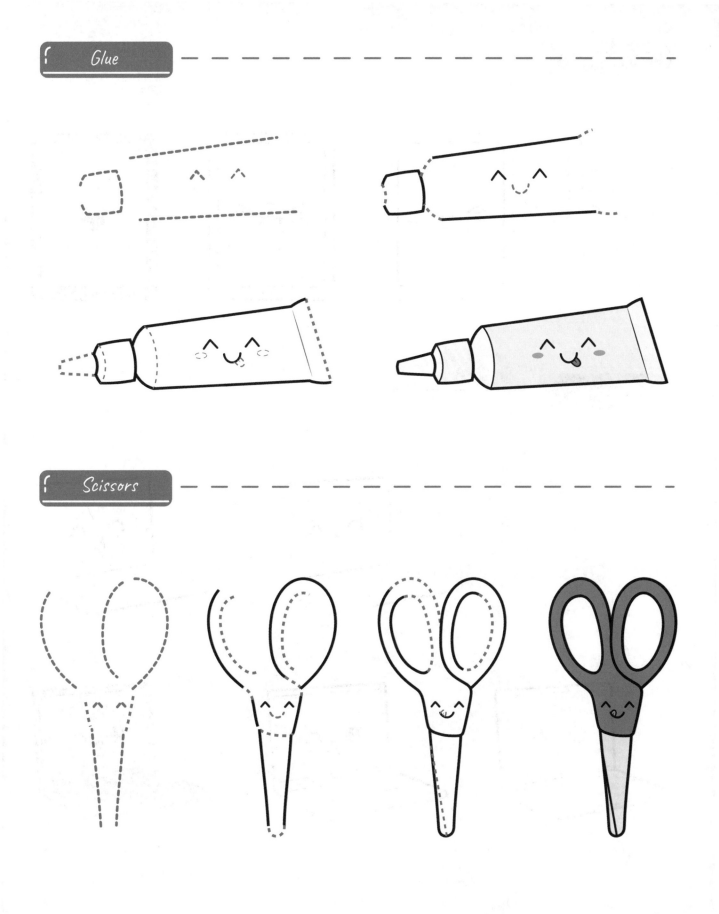

Tablet

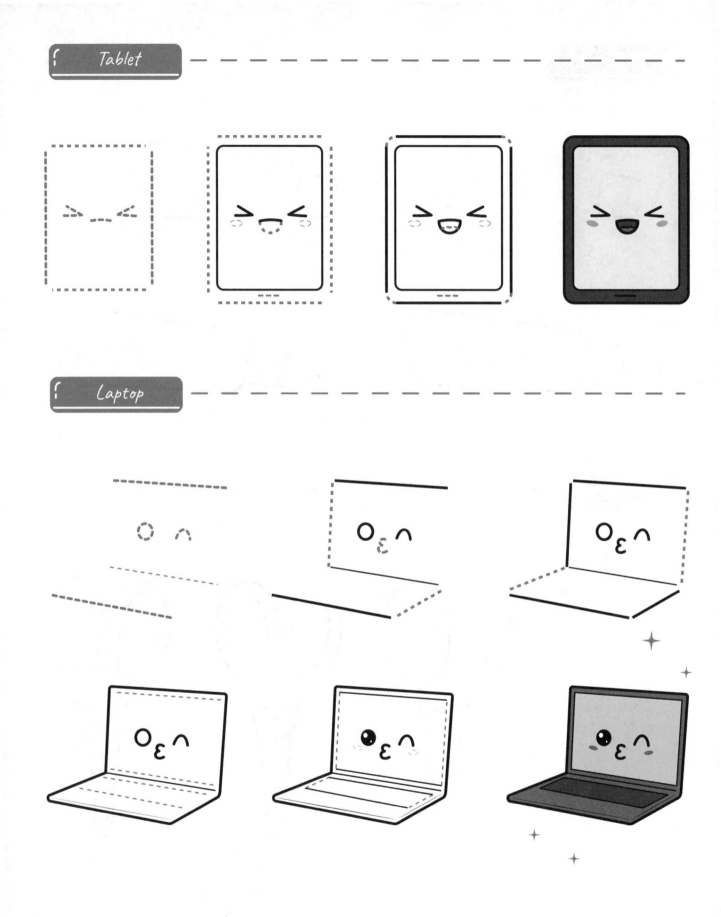

Laptop

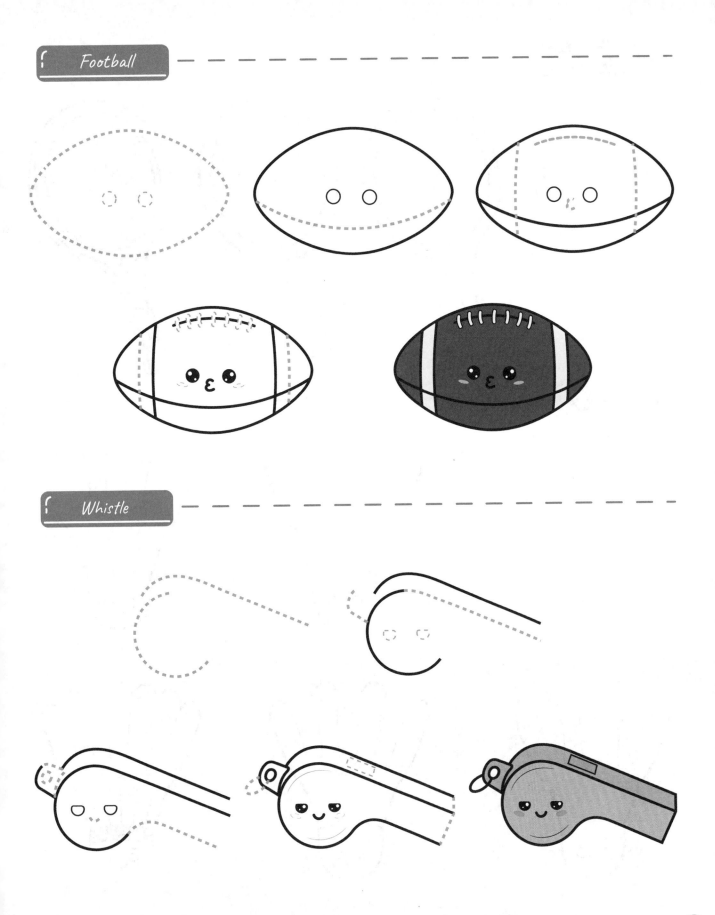

Football

Whistle

Birdie

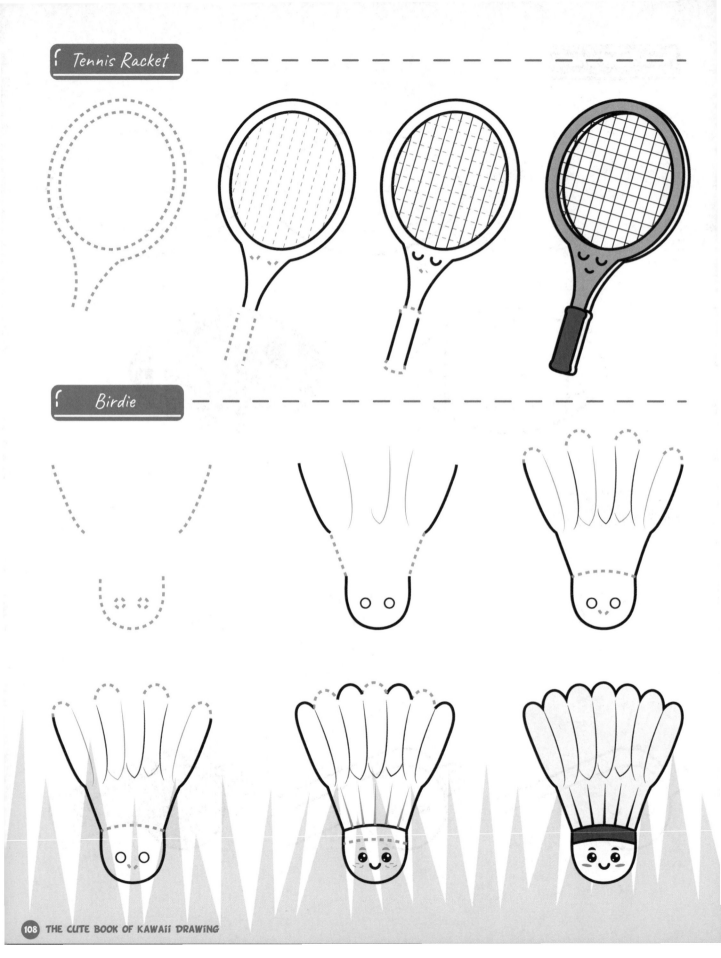

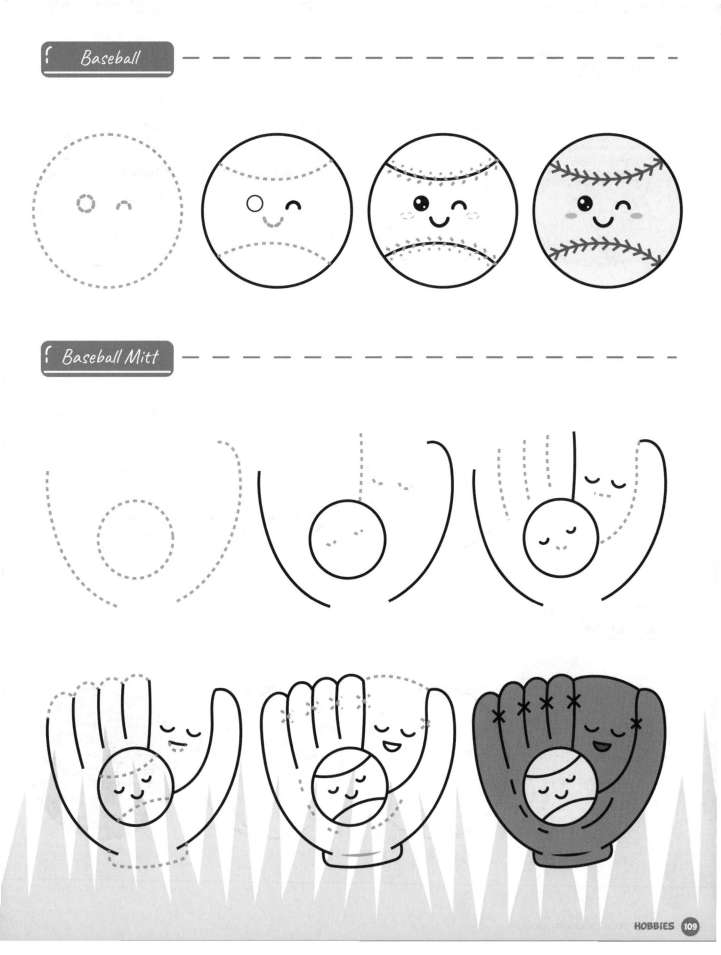

Baseball Mitt

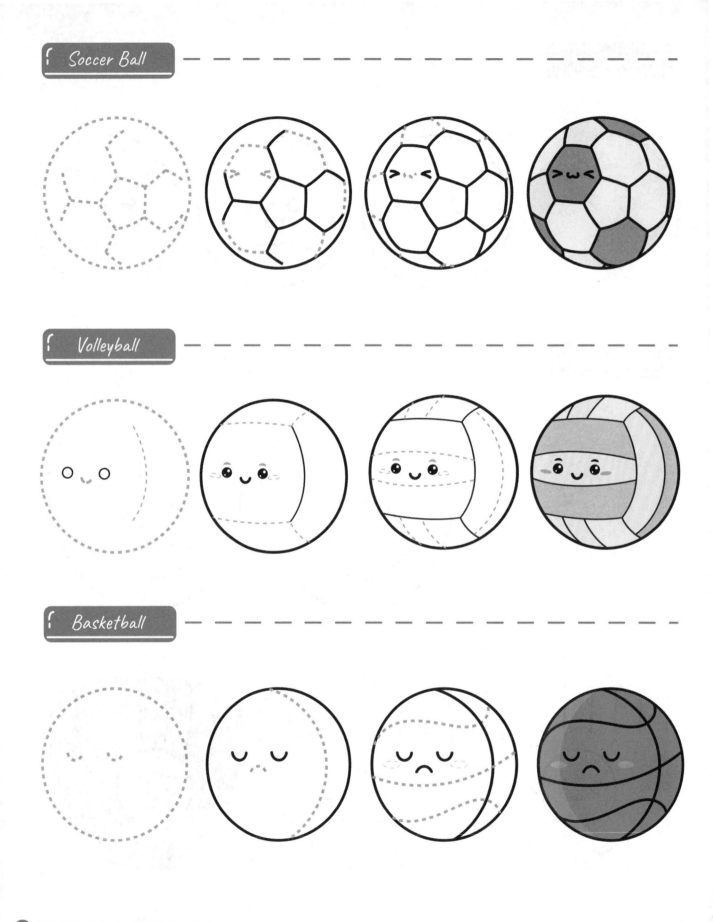

Soccer Ball

Volleyball

Basketball

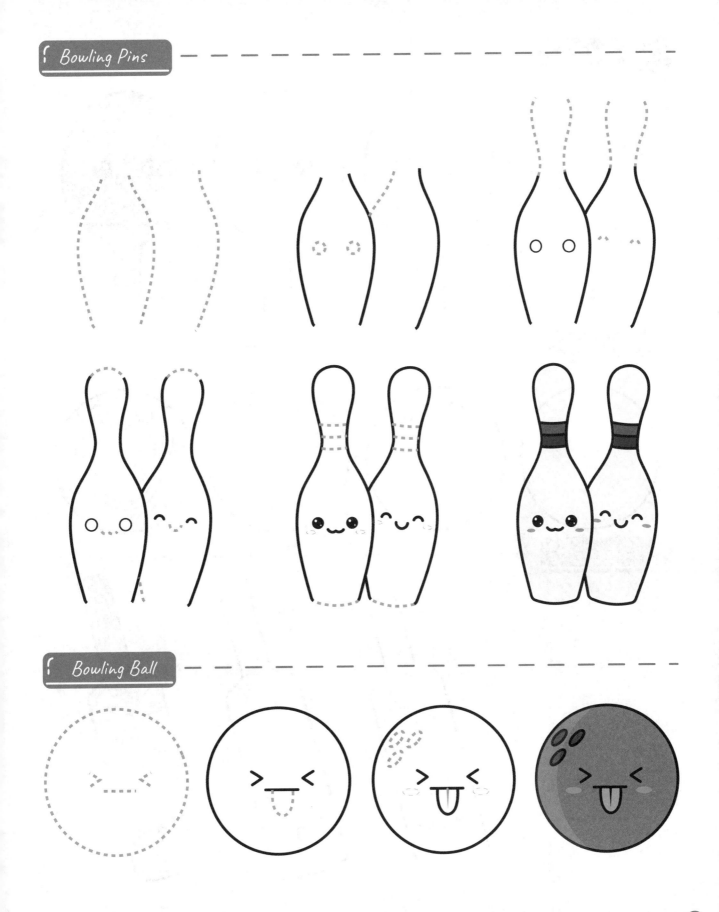

Bowling Ball

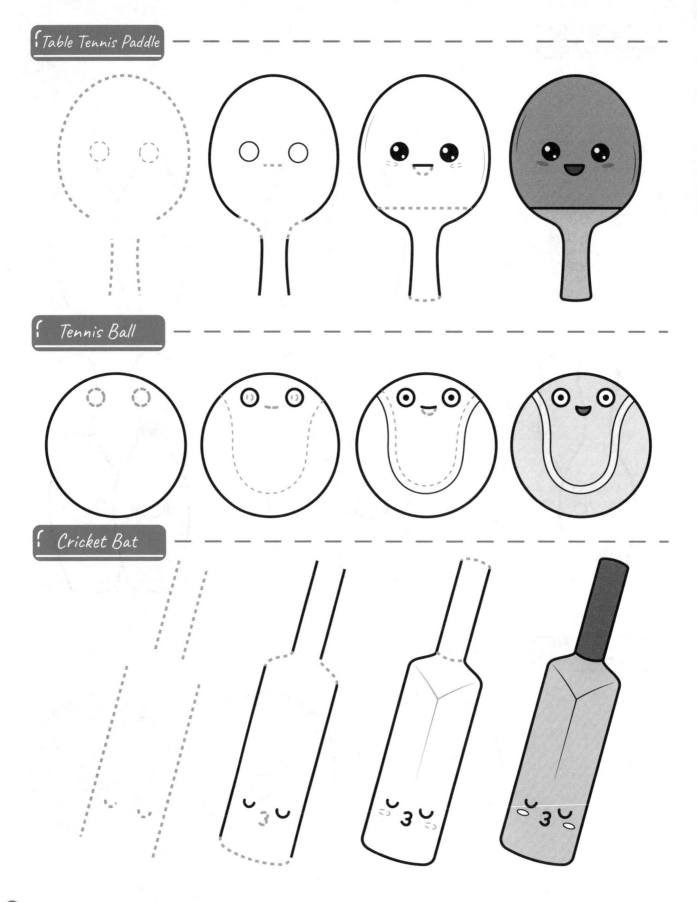

Table Tennis Paddle

Tennis Ball

Cricket Bat

ANIMAL FRIENDS

Lion

Mouse

Snake

Lizard

Frog

Pony

Cat

Hedgehog

Groundhog

Shiba Inu

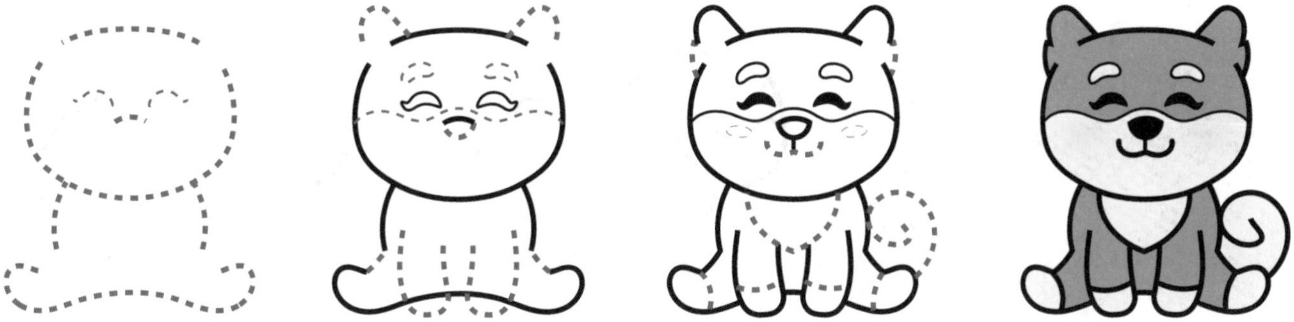

Husky

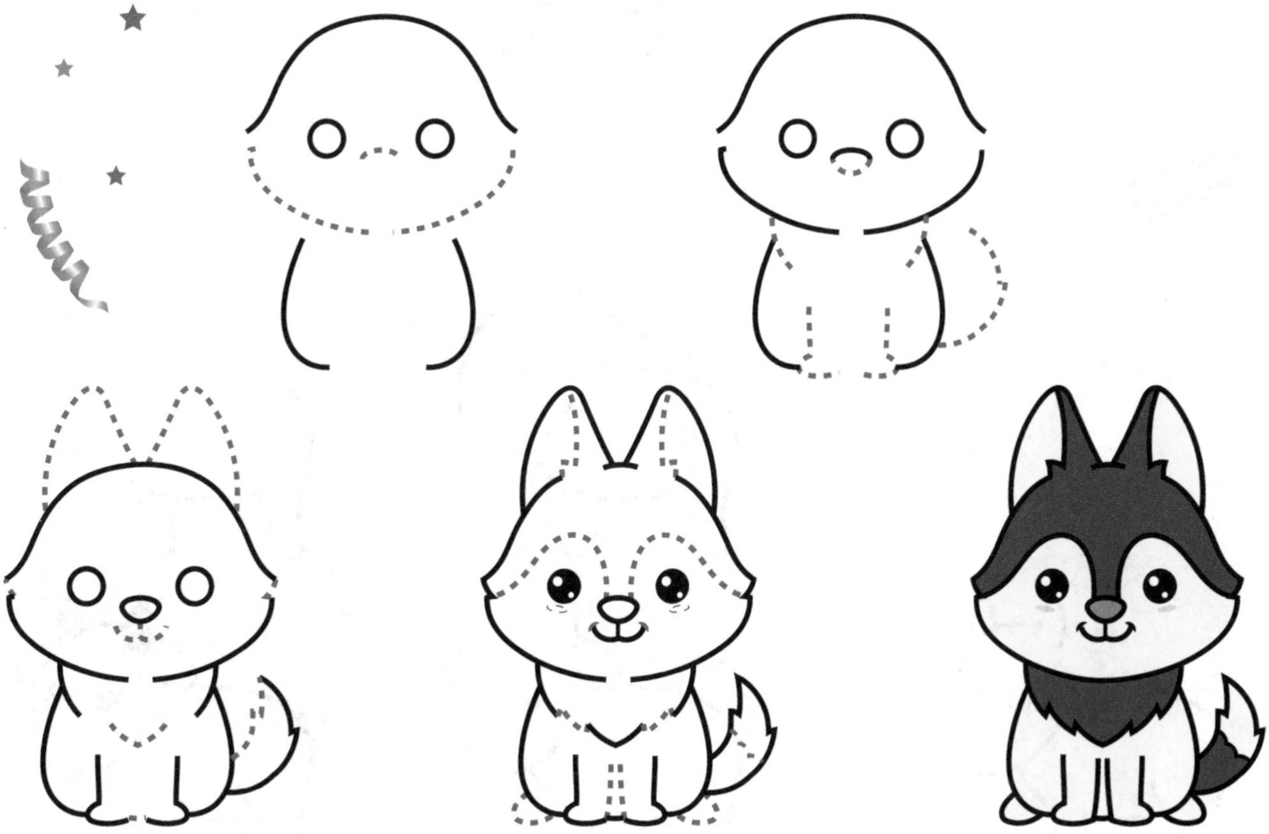

Sheep

Goat

Cow

Deer

Panda

Elephant

Squirrel

Bear

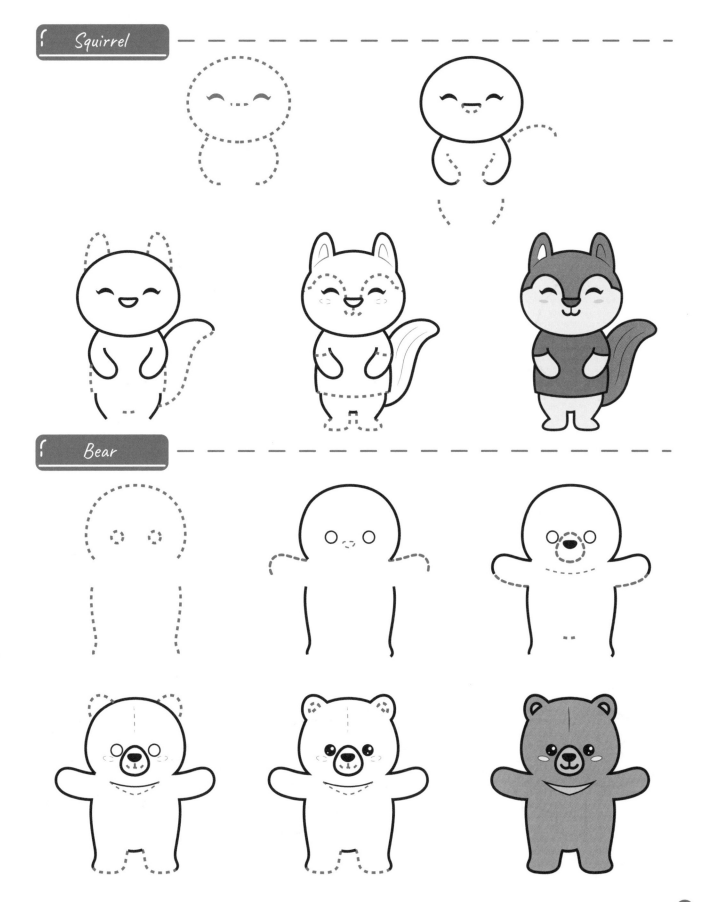

Beaver

Rhino

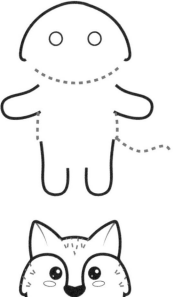

Sloth

Zebra

CUTE HOLIDAYS

Santa ‑

Christmas Tree ‑

Gingerbread Man

Present

Stocking

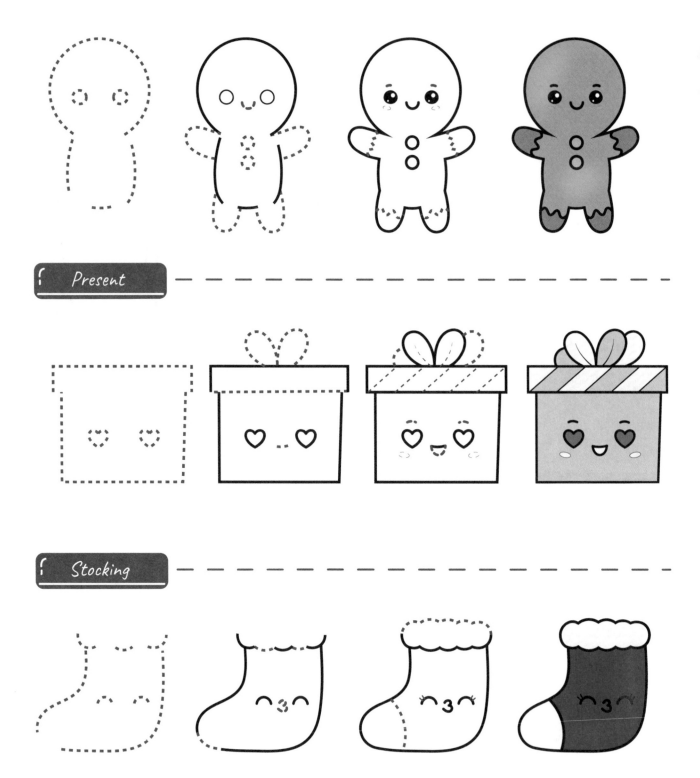

Christmas Elf

Snowman

Reindeer

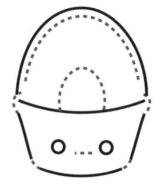

Easter Chick

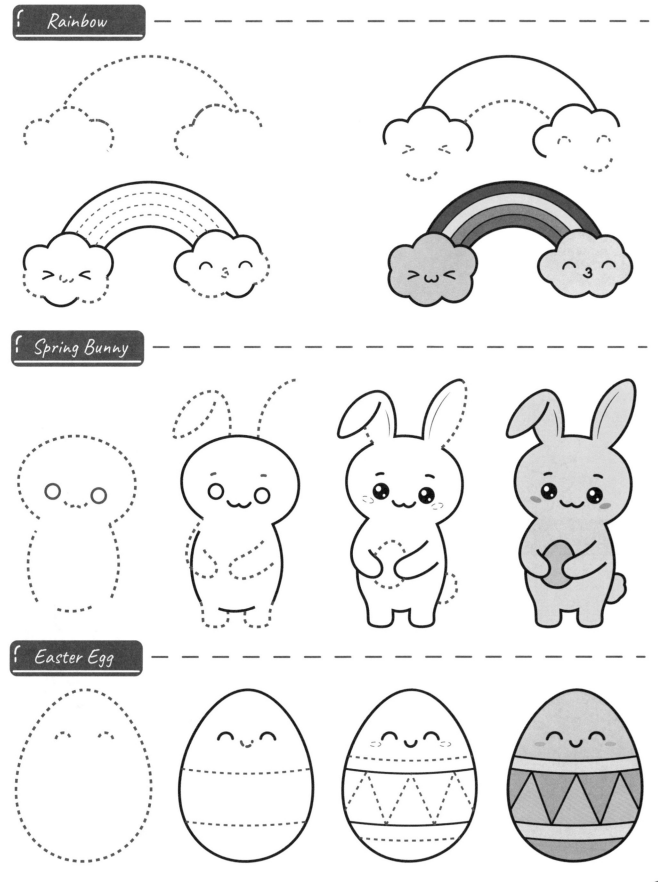

Rainbow

Spring Bunny

Easter Egg

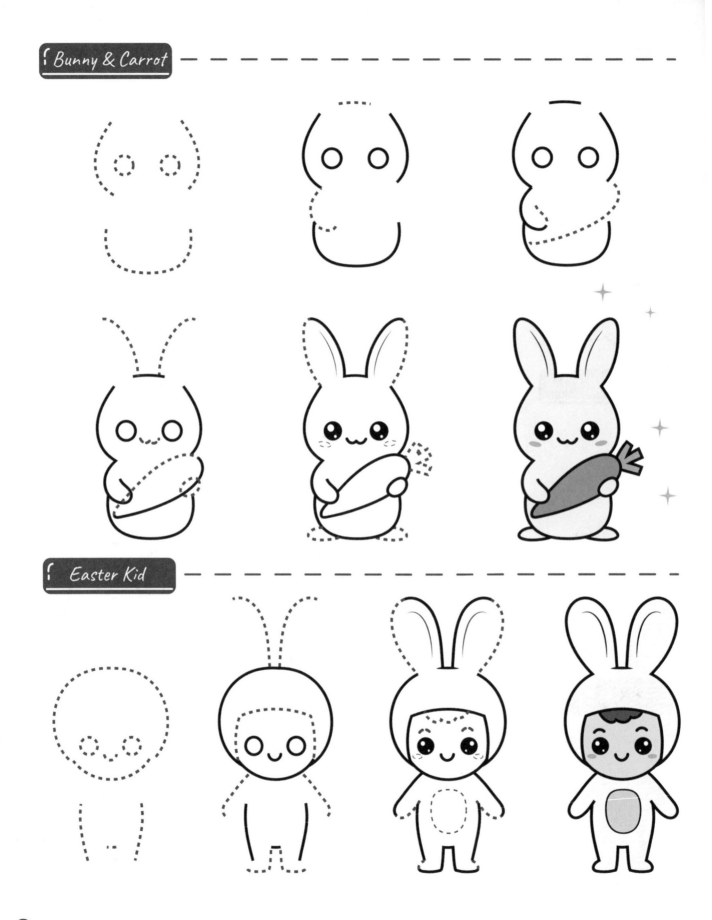

Easter Kid

Carrot

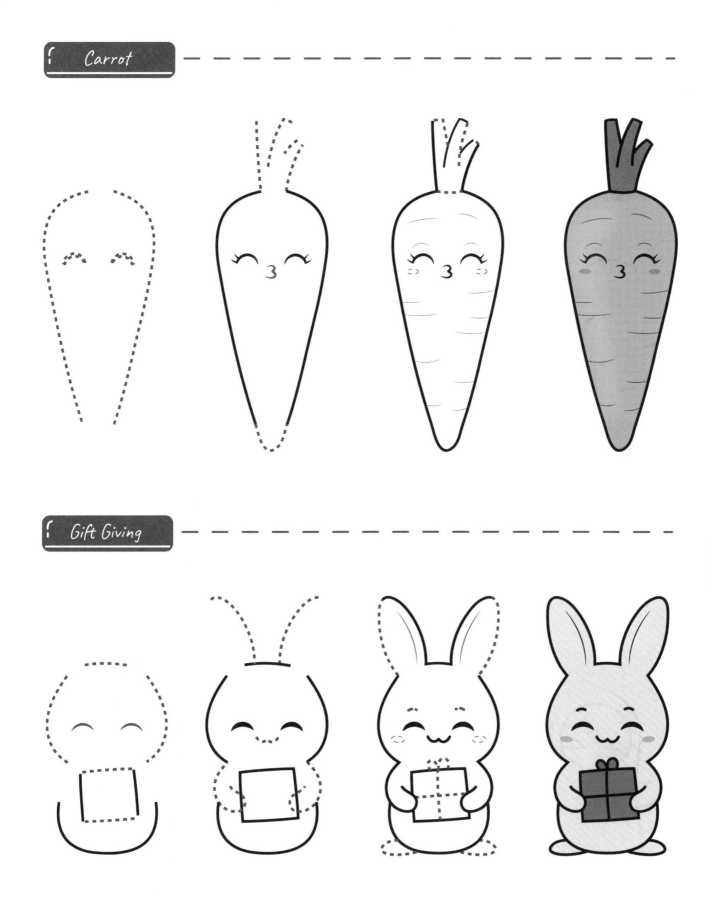

Gift Giving

Witch Hat

Grim Reaper

Spider

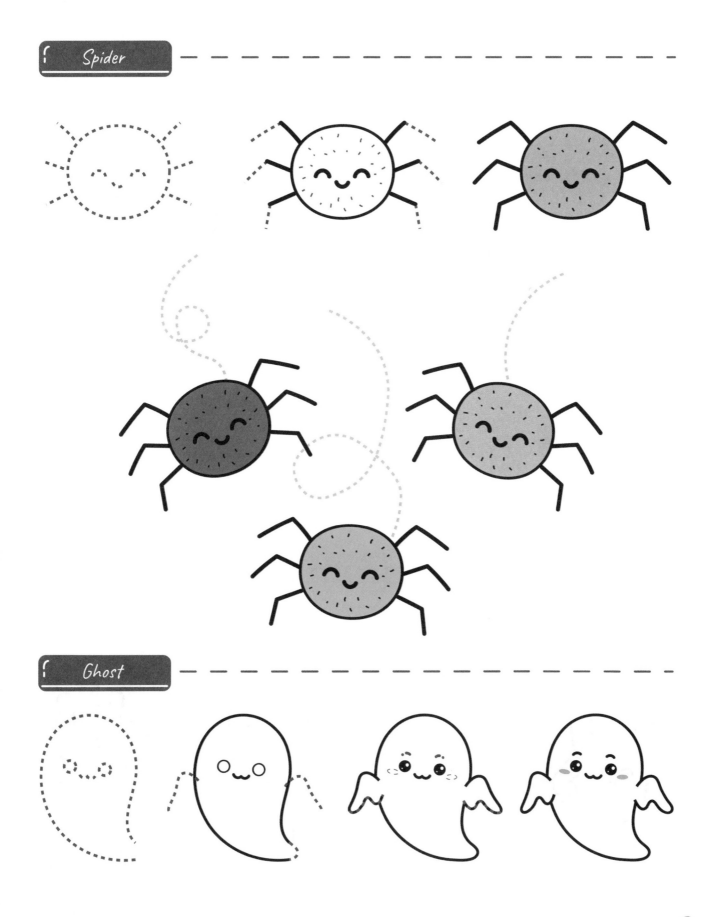

Ghost

Tombstone

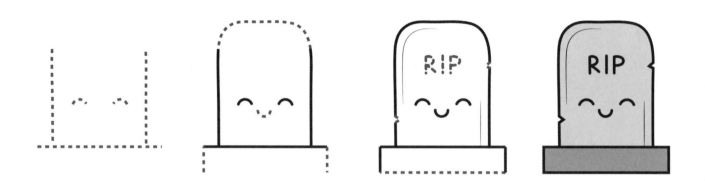

Zombie Hand

Bones

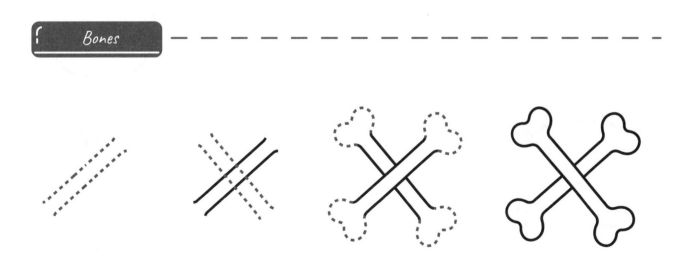

Mummy

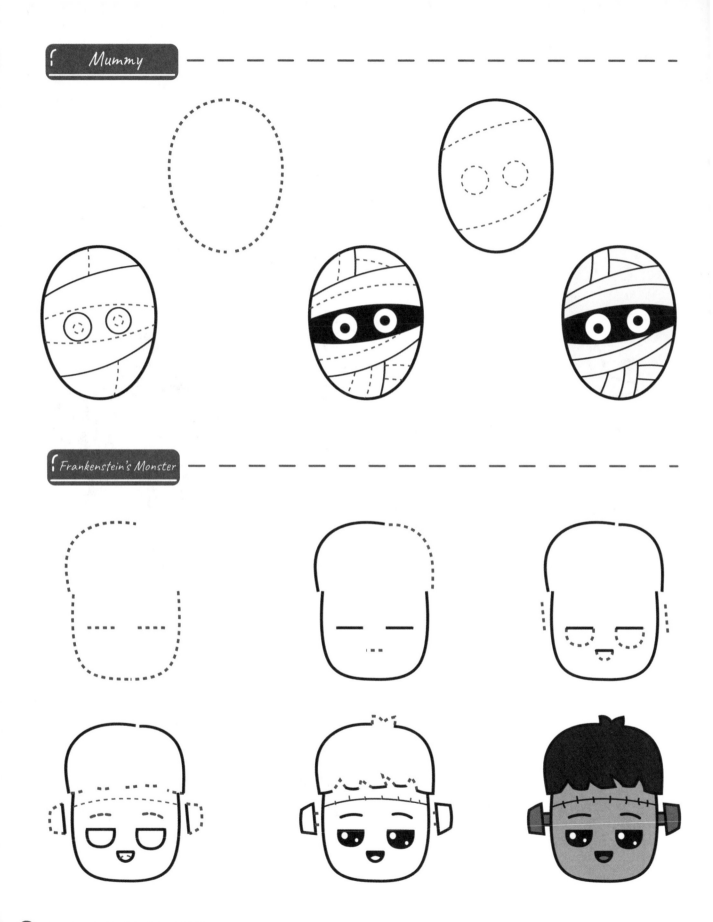

Frankenstein's Monster

Vampire Bat

Vampire

Casket

Black Cat — — — — — — — — — — —

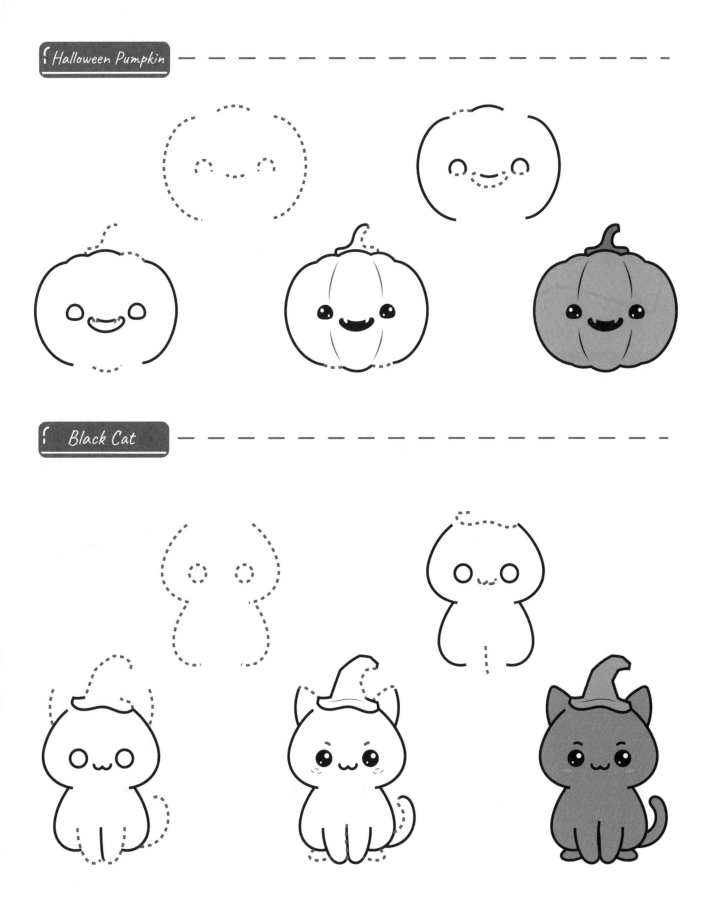

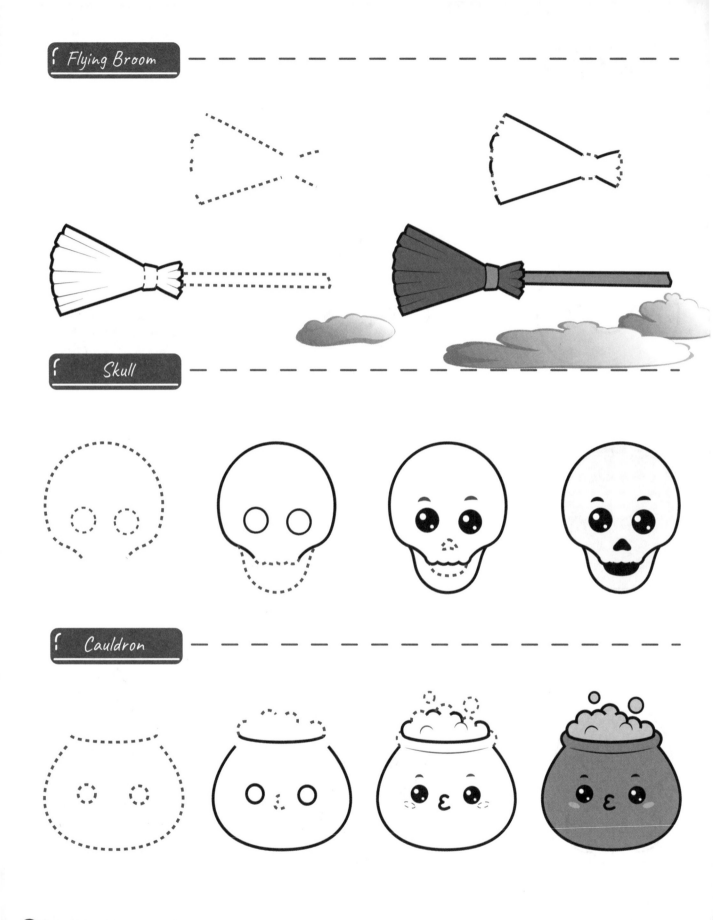

Flying Broom

Skull

Cauldron

Maple Leaf

Oak Leaf

Scarecrow

Acorn

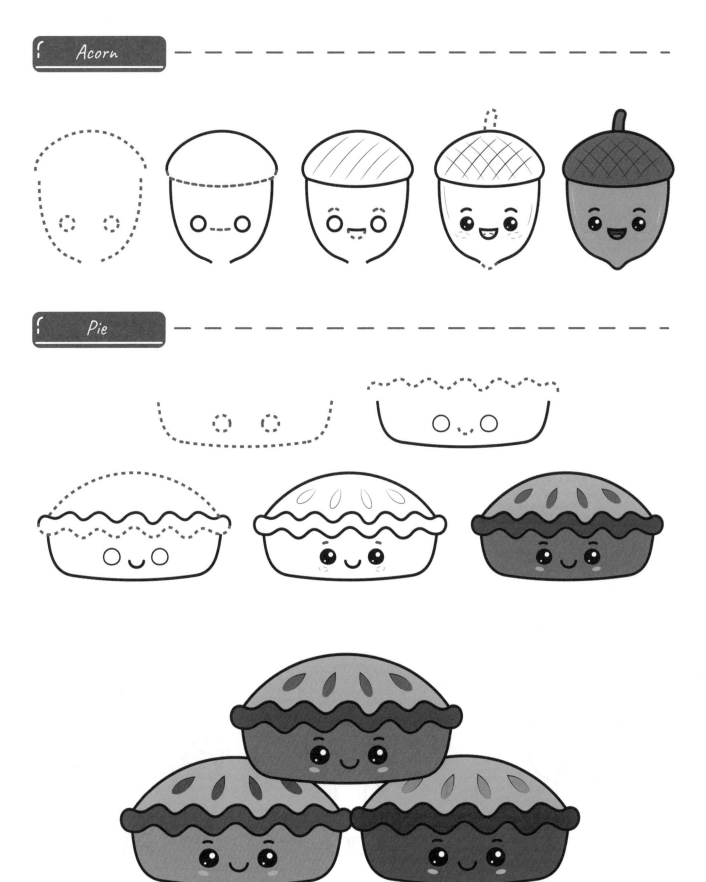

Pie

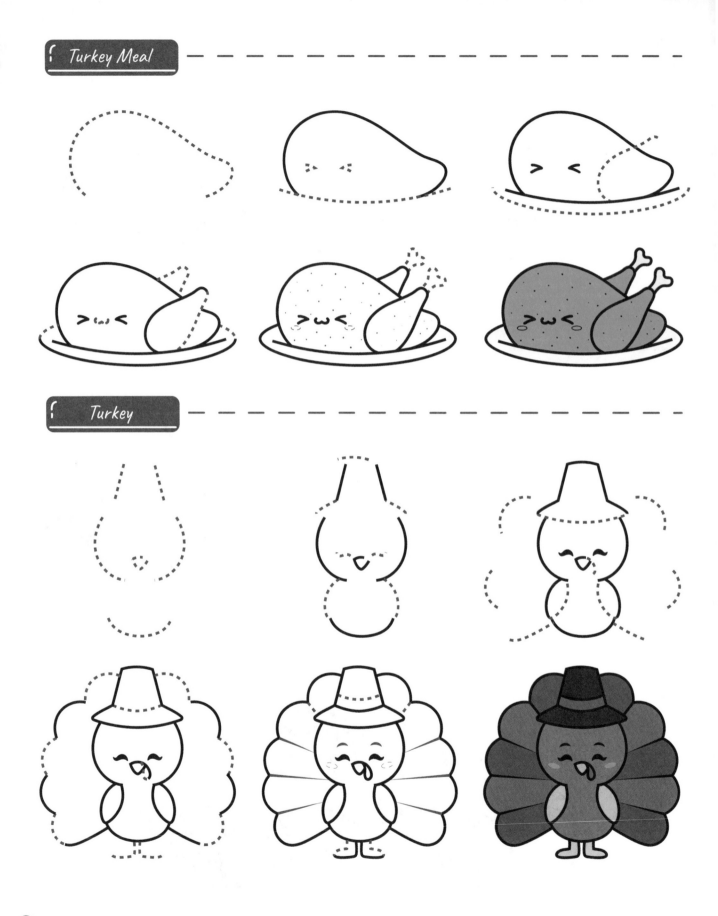

Turkey Meal

Turkey

TASTY TREATS

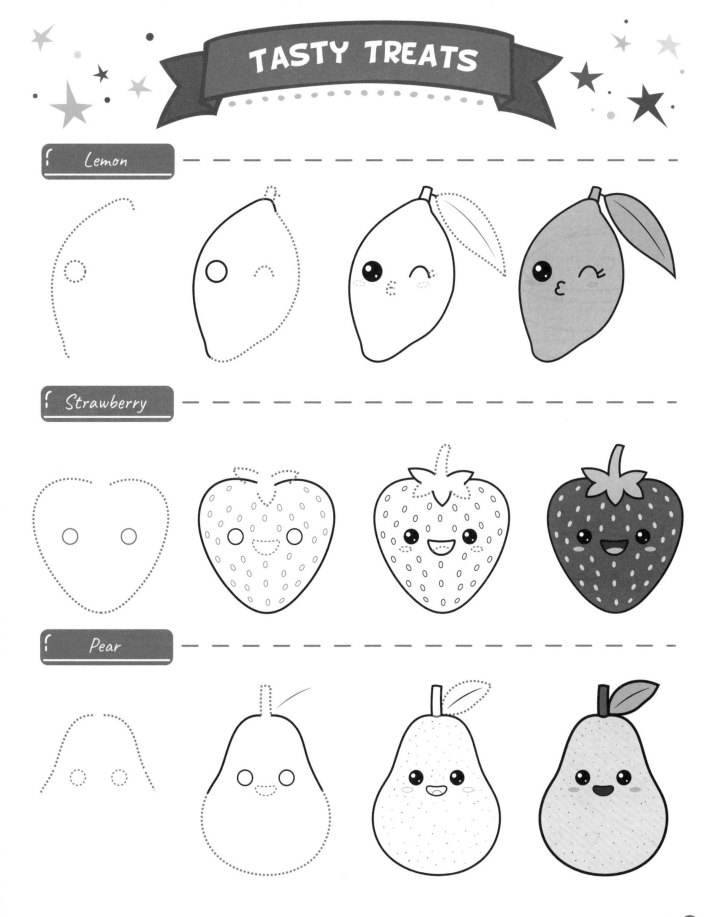

Lemon

Strawberry

Pear

Pretzel

Cheese

Croissant

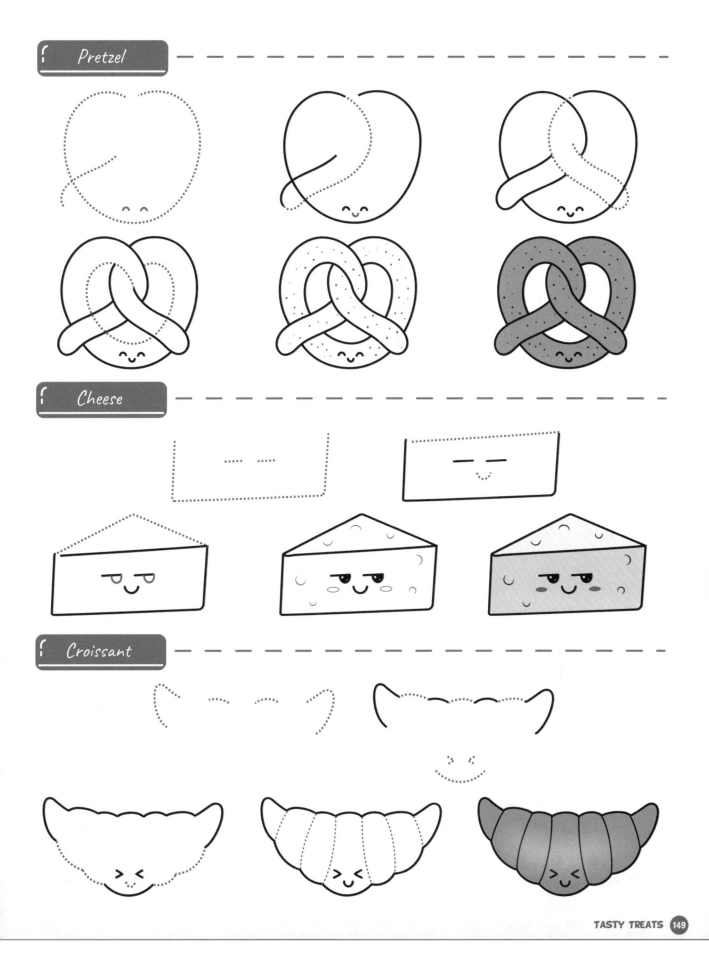

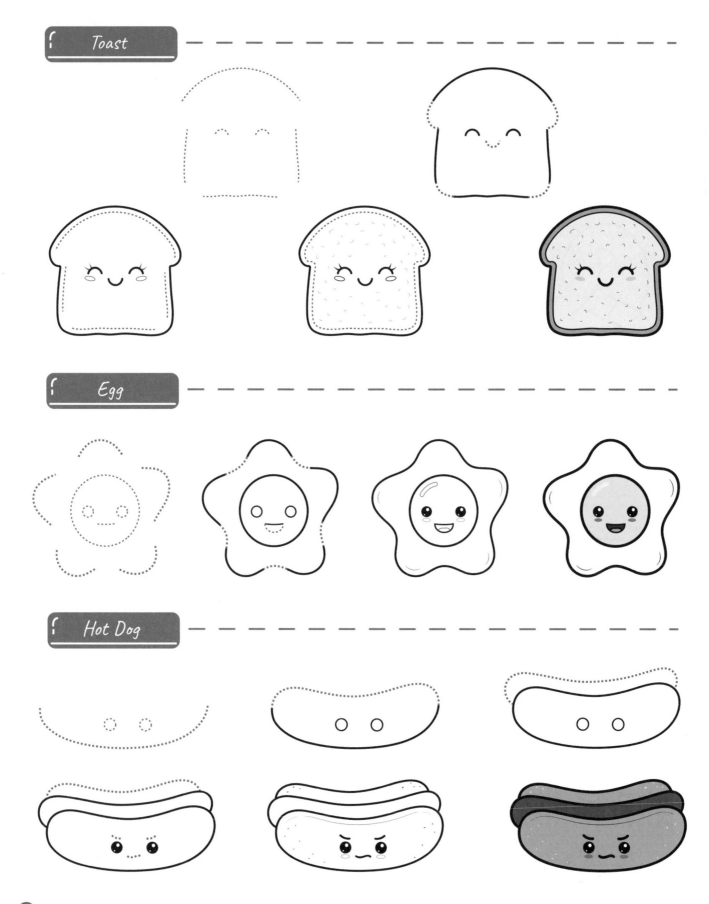

Toast

Egg

Hot Dog

Dumpling

Taco

Sushi

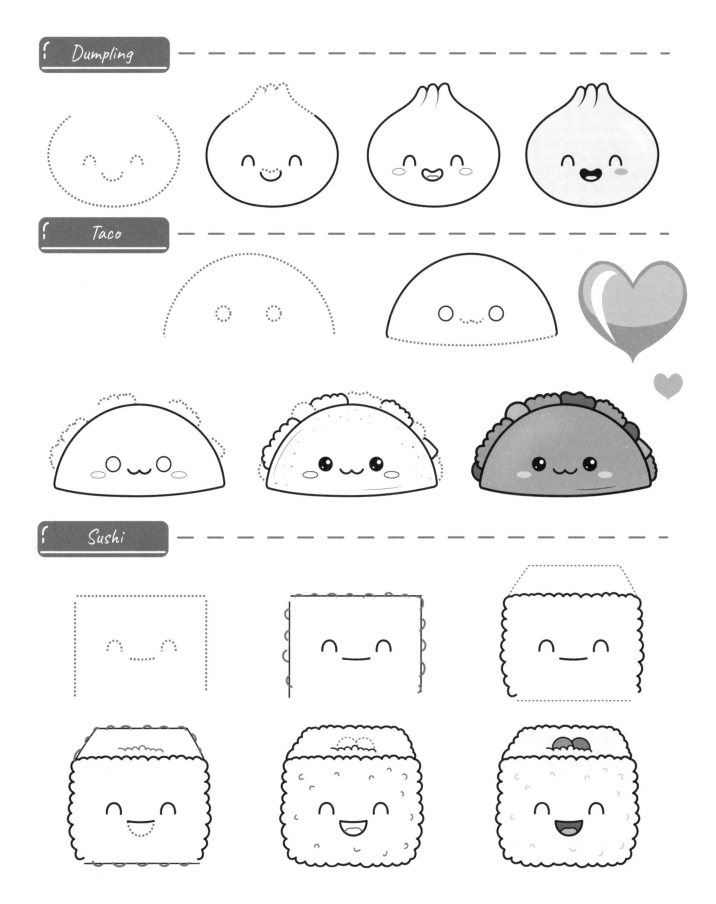

Avocado

Banana

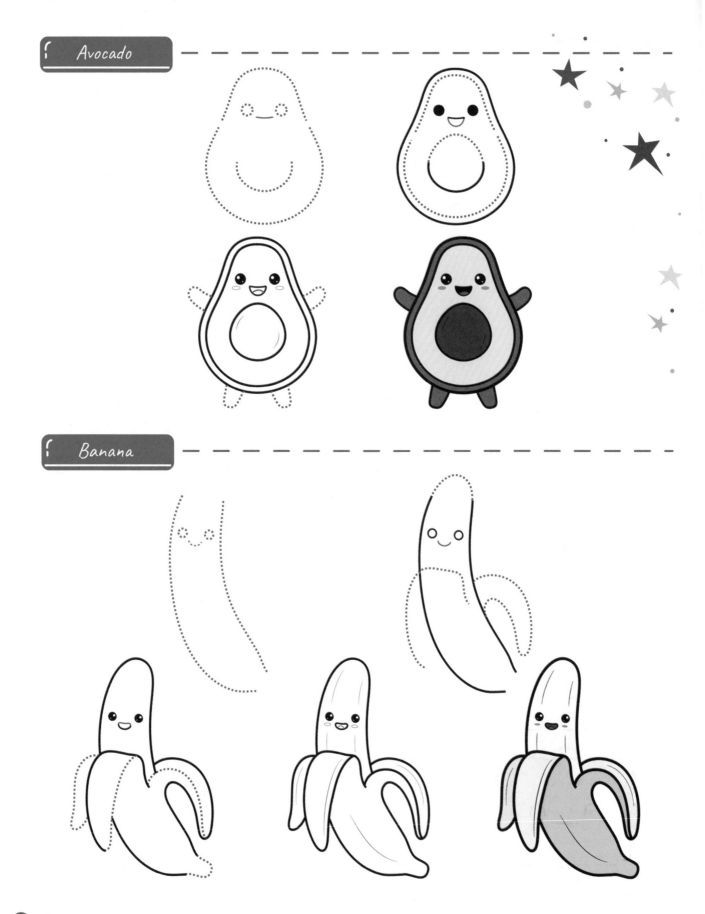

Raspberry

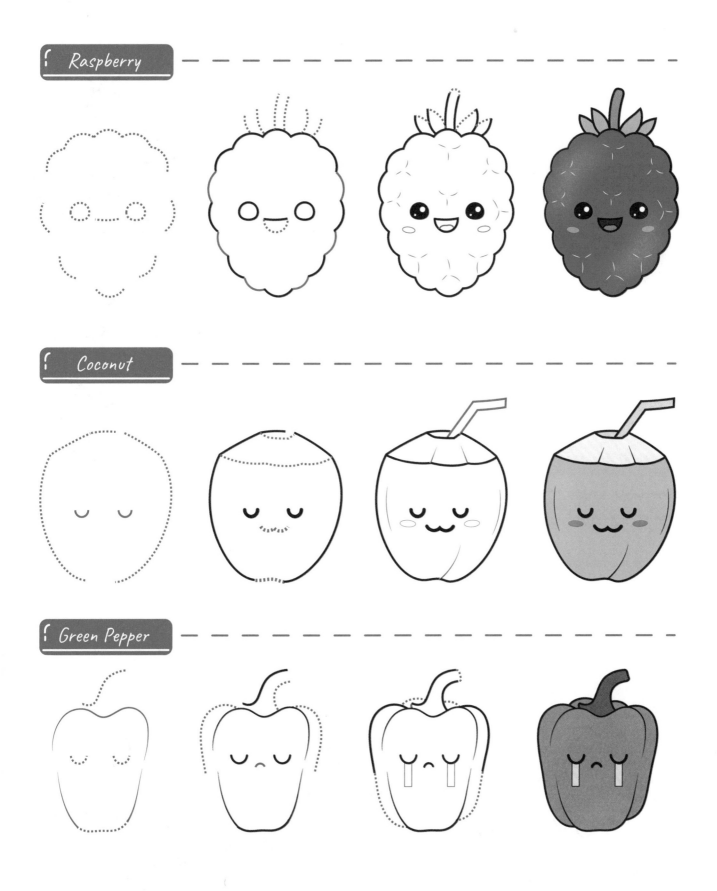

Coconut

Green Pepper

Beet

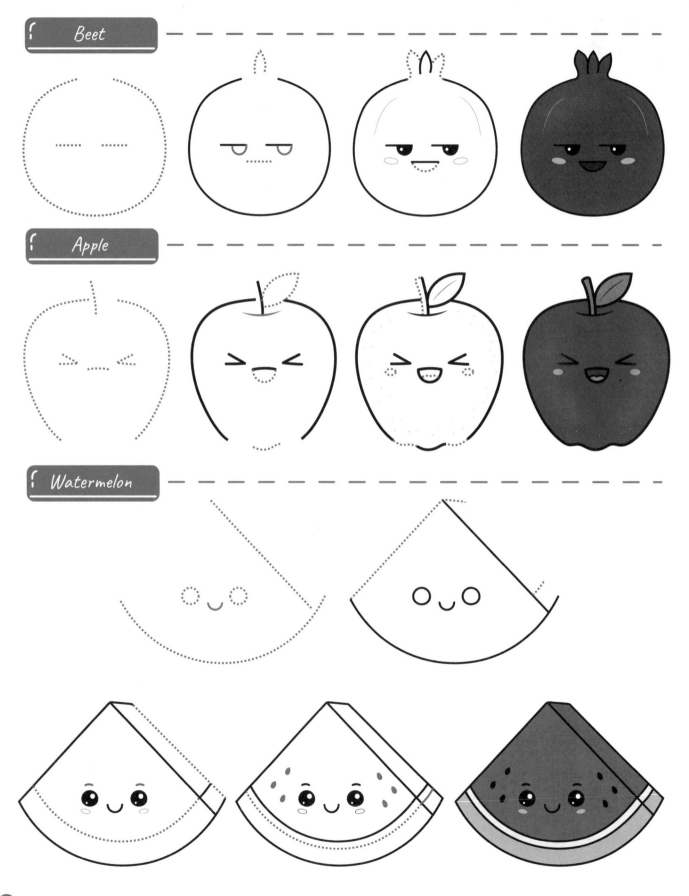

Apple

Watermelon

Honey

Cookie

Flan Cake

Birthday Cake

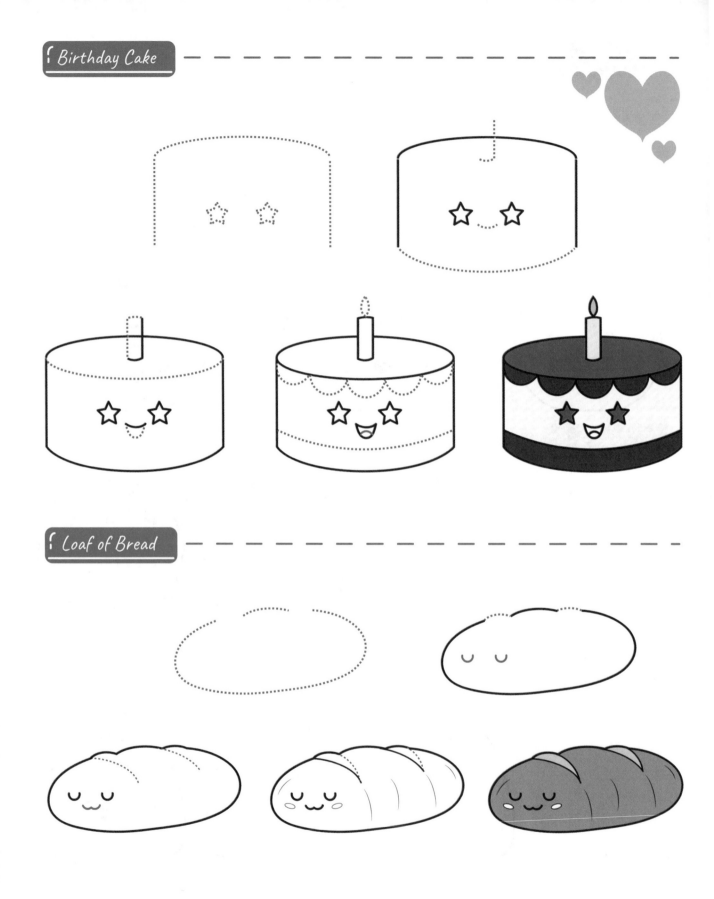

Loaf of Bread

Ice Cream Bar

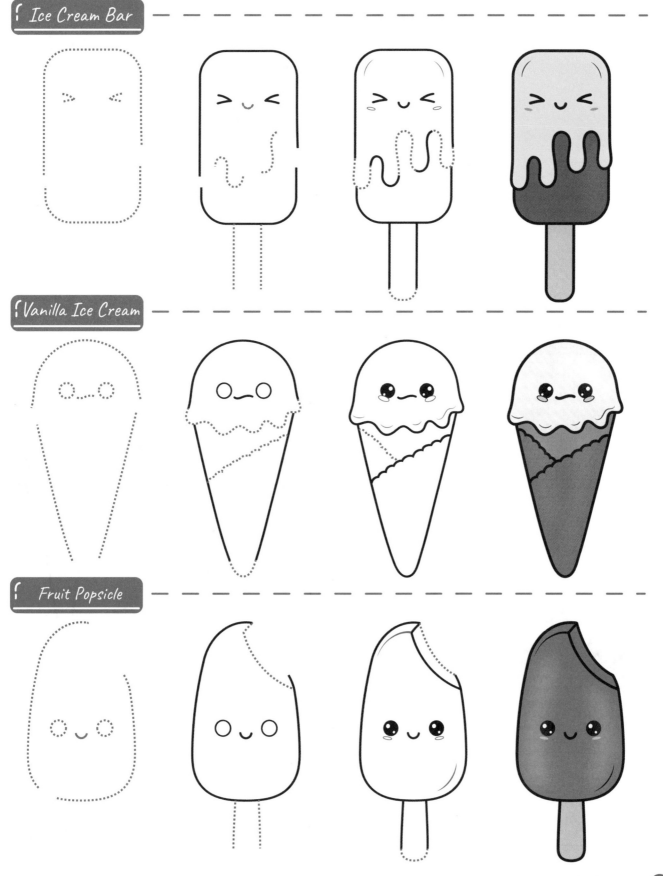

Vanilla Ice Cream

Fruit Popsicle

Muffin

Slice of Cake

Milkshake

Lollipop

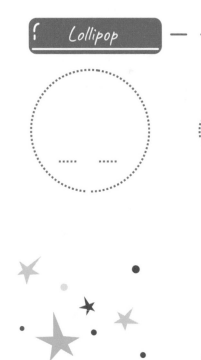

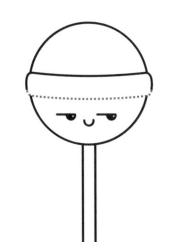

Hard Candy

Macaron

Mochi Balls

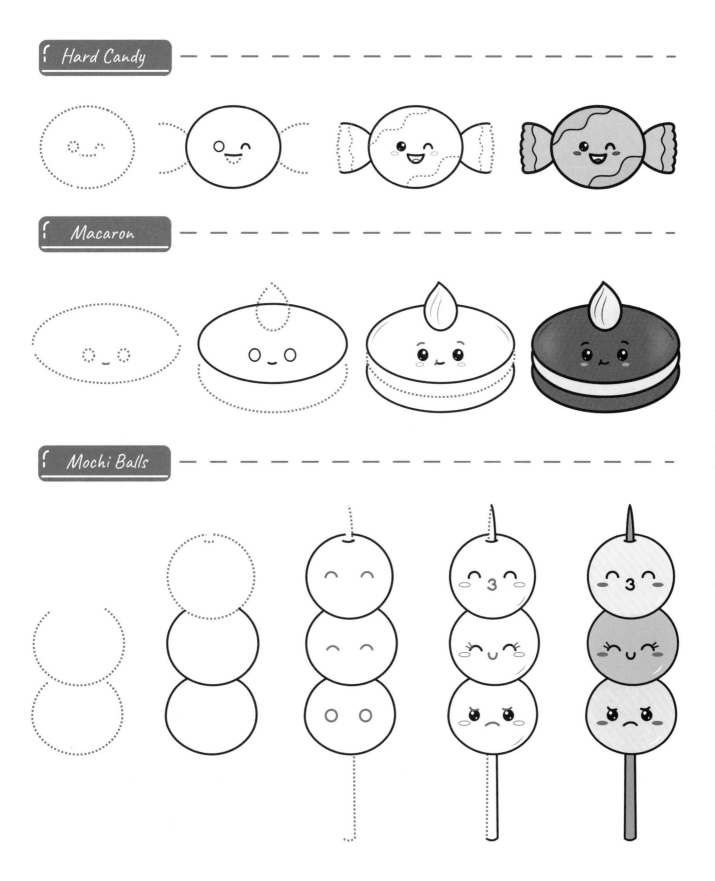

Milk

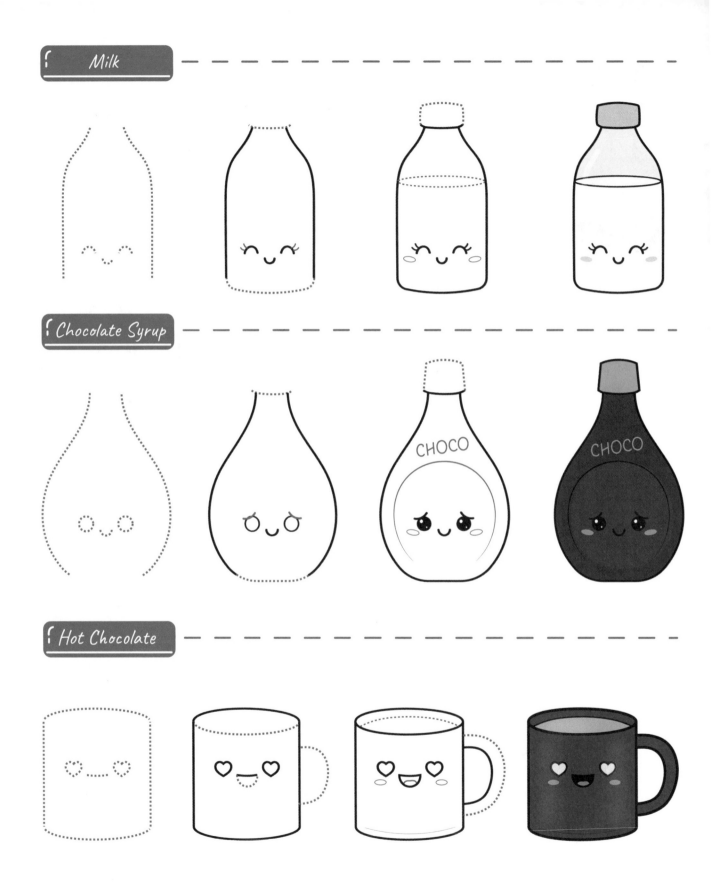

Chocolate Syrup

Hot Chocolate

Hot Sauce

Ramen Bowl

Peanut Butter

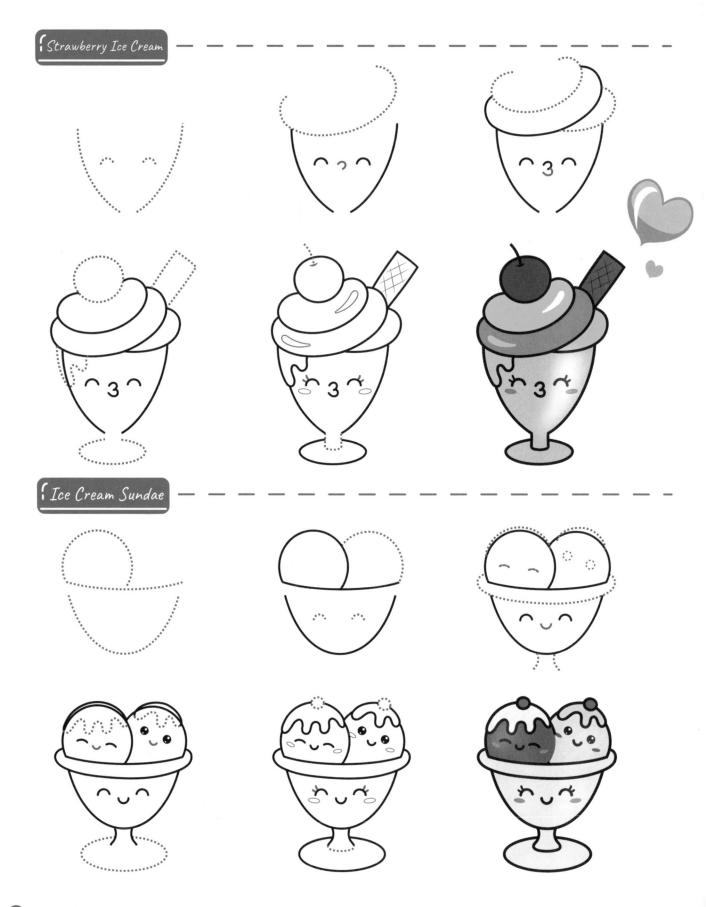

Citrus Cupcake

Birthday Cupcake

Dragonfruit

Mango

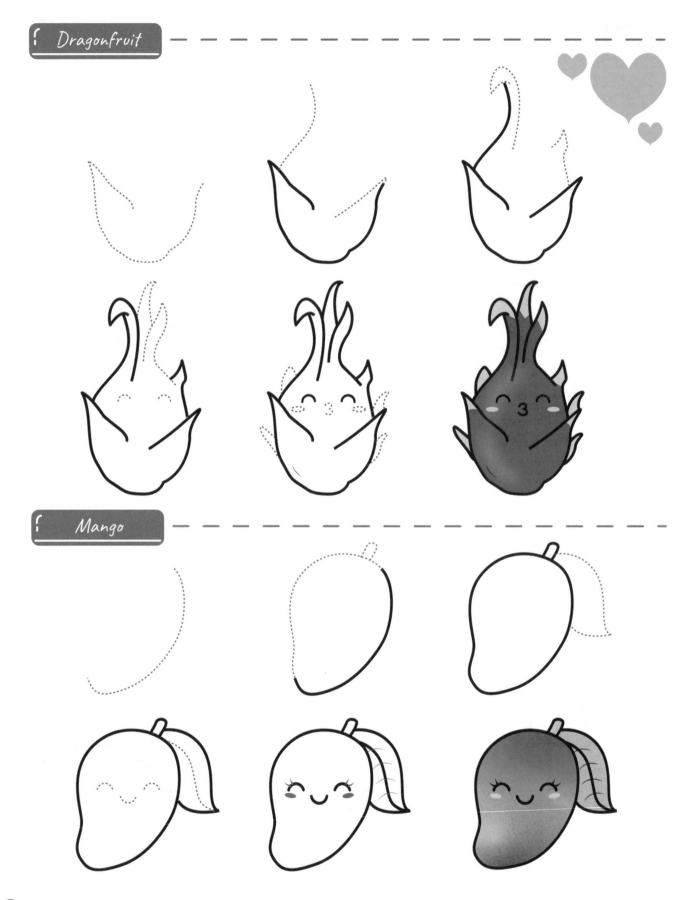

DragonFruit, an imprint of Mango Publishing, publishes high-quality children's books to inspire a love of lifelong learning in readers. DragonFruit publishes a variety of titles for kids, including children's picture books, nonfiction series, toddler activity books, pre-K activity books, science and education titles, and ABC books. Beautiful and engaging, our books celebrate diversity, spark curiosity, and capture the imaginations of parents and children alike.

Mango Publishing, established in 2014, publishes an eclectic list of books by diverse authors. We were named the Fastest Growing Independent Publisher by Publishers Weekly in 2019 and 2020. Our success is bolstered by our main goal, which is to publish high quality books that will make a positive impact in people's lives.

Our readers are our most important resource; we value your input, suggestions, and ideas. We'd love to hear from you—after all, we are publishing books for you!

Please stay in touch with us and follow us at:

Instagram: @dragonfruitkids
Facebook: Mango Publishing
Twitter: @MangoPublishing
LinkedIn: Mango Publishing
Pinterest: Mango Publishing

Sign up for our newsletter at www.mangopublishinggroup.com and receive a free book! Join us on Mango's journey to change publishing, one book at a time.

Woo! Jr. Kids' Activities is passionate about inspiring children to learn through imagination and FUN. That is why we have provided thousands of craft ideas, printables, and teacher resources to over 55 million people since 2008. We are on a mission to produce books that allow kids to build knowledge, express their talent, and grow into creative, compassionate human beings. Elementary education teachers, day care professionals, and parents have come to rely on Woo! Jr. for high-quality, engaging, and innovative content that children LOVE. Our bestselling kids activity books have sold over 300,000 copies worldwide.